ELI • 229

Raiders from New France

North American Forest Warfare Tactics, 17th–18th Centuries

RENÉ CHARTRAND

ILLUSTRATED BY ADAM HOOK

Series editor Martin Windrow

OSPREY PUBLISHING
Bloomsbury Publishing Plc
PO Box 883, Oxford, OX1 9PL, UK
1385 Broadway, 5th Floor, New York, NY 10018, USA
E-mail: info@ospreypublishing.com
www.ospreypublishing.com

OSPREY is a trademark of Osprey Publishing Ltd

First published in Great Britain in 2019

A catalog record for this book is available from the British Library

ISBN: PB 9781472833501; eBook 9781472833709; ePDF 9781472833693; XML 9781472833686

19 20 21 22 23 10 9 8 7 6 5 4 3 2 1

Editor: Martin Windrow
Index by Fionbar Lyons
Typeset by PDQ Digital Media Solutions, Bungay, UK
Printed and bound in India by Replika Press Private Ltd.

Osprey Publishing supports the Woodland Trust, the UK's leading woodland conservation charity.

To find out more about our authors and books, visit **www.ospreypublishing.com**. Here you will find extracts, author interviews, details of forthcoming events, and the option to sign up for our newsletter.

AUTHOR'S NOTE

The denomination "Canadian" in this text is the literal translation of *Canadien*, commonly used up to the 20th century for persons of French roots born in Canada, and later known as French-Canadians.
The denomination "Indian" has recently declined in use in North America. The terms "Indigenous" and "First Nations" are now officially used by the government of Canada to identify those peoples, who currently represent 5 percent of the country's population. (Incidentally, their numbers are growing four times faster than the national average. By comparison, the "Native American" population of the USA stands at about 1.7 percent of the total, and is said to be declining.)

Most of the illustrations in this book, which are largely unknown in the anglophone world, were published in Quebec's francophone media a century or more ago – notably the small drawings by the prolific Edmond J. Massicotte, who illustrated many historical works. We have made an effort here to make a few of them known to a larger audience.

ACKNOWLEDGMENTS

The author acknowledges the very kind assistance given by Francis Back, Russel Bouchard, André Gousse, Kevin Gélinas, the National Historic sites of Parks Canada, the Archives nationales de France, the Archives nationales du Québec, Library and Archives Canada, as well as private collections. All the material in this book could never have come together without the fine editorial work and coordination of Martin Windrow and Brianne Bellio at Osprey. To one and all, we express our deepest gratitude.

ARTIST'S NOTE

Reader may care to note that the original paintings from which the color plates in this book were prepared are available for private sale. All reproduction copyright whatsoever is retained by the publisher. All inquiries should be addressed to:

Scorpio, 158 Mill Road, Hailsham, East Sussex BN27 2SH, UK
scorpiopaintings@btinternet.com

The publishers regret that they can enter into no correspondence upon this matter.

CONTENTS

RAIDERS FROM NEW FRANCE

NORTH AMERICAN FOREST WARFARE TACTICS, 17th-18th CENTURIES

INTRODUCTION

During what the anglophone world generally calls the "French and Indian Wars," the tactics of surprise attacks and raids launched from within New France kept the Anglo-American colonies on the Atlantic seaboard in a defensive posture for three-quarters of a century. Meanwhile, by mounting audacious expeditions, the French settlers – though less numerous by a factor of ten – came to dominate trade in immense wilderness areas from the Gulf of St Lawrence down to the Gulf of Mexico, and explored as far west as the Rocky Mountains. The object of this study is simply to explain how this came about, and to identify the leaders who devised and promoted the tactics that had such extraordinary geo-strategic consequences.

The challenge faced by New France was not only to keep the faster-growing Anglo-American colonies contained, but also, when diplomacy and trade agreements failed, to vanquish hostile First Nations. Success in both objectives was achieved by the creation of a superior fighting force with a longer reach. There were no manuals describing "how to" fight in the North American wilderness; but by collating various memoirs and documentary records, and by analyzing actual expeditions as well as the important material-culture aspects, we can discern a fascinating picture. Thanks to visionary officers who formed and maintained close relations with friendly First Nations, a successful Canadian European/Indigenous tactical doctrine became firmly rooted.

THE BEGINNINGS

Champlain, Frontenac, and La Barre, 1608–85

That French permanent settlements in North America became a reality during the 17th century was thanks largely to Samuel de Champlain.[1] His establishment

1 Samuel de Champlain (1567–1635) was a remarkable navigator and explorer turned diplomat, trader and soldier, who made more than 20 trans-Atlantic crossings. From 1620 he was governor of New France in all but formal title, and he was appointed lieutenant-governor by Cardinal Richelieu in 1633.

in Acadia (present-day Nova Scotia) in 1604 was soon followed in 1608 by another at Quebec, which became the capital city of New France, and as decades passed other settlements such as Trois-Rivières (1634) and Montreal (1642) were founded further up the St Lawrence River.

At the outset, the French had befriended the Huron (Wendat) First Nation, and in 1609–10 Champlain and a few companions won battles against the redoubtable Iroquois by the use of firearms. In the late 1630s the Iroquois themselves obtained firearms from the Dutch and English colonies to the south, and by 1649 the Iroquois confederacy had largely wiped out or driven off the Hurons and then turned their attention to the French settlements. Parties of warriors would suddenly attack, kill or kidnap, then simply vanish into the forest. Colonists in Montreal and Trois-Rivières had to go armed whenever they left their homes.

By May 1660 the Iroquois menace had increased to such an extent that a detachment of 17 soldiers in a small fort were overwhelmed. The French colony was in fear of being wiped out until, in 1665, King Louis XIV sent out the regular Carignan-Salières Regiment to keep the Iroquois at bay. After both winter and summer military expeditions, the Iroquois agreed to a peace treaty in 1668, though relations remained tense. While the Carignan-Salières then returned to France, some hundreds of officers and men chose to remain as settlers. By now the French had become heavily involved in the lucrative fur trade, whose expansion demanded ever more extensive exploration of the continent's interior.

OPPOSITE
This engraving titled "Canadian wearing snowshoes going to war on the snow," from 1722, is the only known contemporary image of a late 17th–early 18th century Canadian militiaman on campaign. It is in Volume 1 of La Potherie's work, where he describes the 1696–97 conquest of British Newfoundland in which 124 Canadian raiders played a leading role. Some features are curiously rendered by a European engraver baffled by unfamiliar North American items such as snowshoes, moccasins, *mitasses*, beaded pouches, a flapped cap and *capot*. The musket's exaggerated buttstock hints at one of the "buccaneer" weapons occasionally seen in Canada. (Print after Bacqueville de La Potherie's *Histoire de l'Amérique septentrionale*, 1722; courtesy Library and Archives Canada, C10605)

Regions of North America claimed by colonial nations, late 17th to mid-18th century. (From Lawler's *Essentials of American History*, 1902; author's photo)

Spirited impression of the last stand of Dollard des Ormeaux, commander of the weak Montreal garrison, who was killed with 16 companions when a small fort at Long Sault on the Ottawa River was overrun by an Iroquois war party in May 1660. The chronicler Dollier de Casson writes that the heavy casualties suffered by the Iroquois deterred them from attacking Montreal itself. (Print after R. Bombled; private collection, author's photo)

In 1672, Louis de Buade, Comte de Frontenac (1622–98), arrived in Quebec city as governor-general of New France. He was a career soldier who, under the great Marshal Turenne, had risen to an appointment as lieutenant-general when only 26 years old, and had later served the Venetian Republic in Crete until it was overwhelmed by the Ottoman Turks in 1669.

When Frontenac arrived at Quebec there were barely 65 soldiers in New France, including his own 20 guardsmen, but he quickly organized a staff with some of the retired officers. He was deeply impressed by North America, and on November 2, 1672, he wrote to Minister Jean-Baptiste Colbert that nothing was "so magnificent as the site of Quebec; this town cannot be better positioned [to] one day become the capital of a great empire." In 1673 Frontenac led an expedition that built a fort at Cataraqui, soon called Fort Frontenac (today Kingston, Ontario). Other forts followed, which became bases for crossing the Great Lakes and thence following the Ohio, Illinois, and Mississippi rivers, and gaining access to the Great Plains. In April 1682, the explorer La Salle would discover that the Mississippi flowed into the Gulf of Mexico, and claimed the whole area for France, naming it Louisiana.

For the defense of New France, Frontenac relied on the armed Canadian Militia, which had been organized into parish companies since 1669. Every able-bodied man aged from 16 to 60 was liable for duty, with officers and sergeants appointed in each parish, and regular company training. The use of firearms for hunting was very widespread, so that many settlers handled them expertly; furthermore, as time passed, increasing numbers were either veterans or the sons of soldiers. Frontenac also noted the remarkable military possibilities of the canoes used for inland trade along North America's extraordinary web of rivers. These could be paddled and *portaged* over enormous distances by Canadian *voyageurs* or *coureur-des-bois* ("travelers" or "woods-runners"), who had become skilled in all aspects of forest-craft.

During Frontenac's administration, although the French colony had hardly any regular troops, the Iroquois generally stayed quiet while exploratory expeditions established new trade links with other First Nations. These too came to know *Onontio* – the French "Father," who ruled for the Great King over the seas. At Cataraqui in July 1673, Frontenac had reassured the assembled chiefs that he wished only friendship, and that he had wanted to meet them because it was important that "a father should know his children and that children know their father." He apologized that he could not understand their language, but he had with him Charles Le Moyne – a leading trader – as his interpreter, "so you will not lose a single word of what I said." Frontenac demonstrated an instinctive skill in the diplomacy required to deal with the First Nations and left a model for his successors (if they had the wit to follow it). Frontenac insisted that some Iroquois chiefs be present in 1673, and this went a long way towards maintaining a peaceful, if rather cool relationship between them and New France.

Ironically, it was Frontenac's impatient temper towards the settlers that eventually got him in trouble with Versailles, which received many complaints about his autocratic ways. (He even used his guardsmen to arrest the governor of Montreal, and a priest who criticized him from the pulpit.) After ten years in Canada, the governor-general was recalled by King Louis XIV. His successor, Joseph-Antoine Lefebvre de La Barre (1622–88), was a naval officer with experience in the West Indies, who arrived in Canada in October 1682 to find a rapidly deteriorating situation. Despite his military weakness, Frontenac had somehow managed to keep the hostile

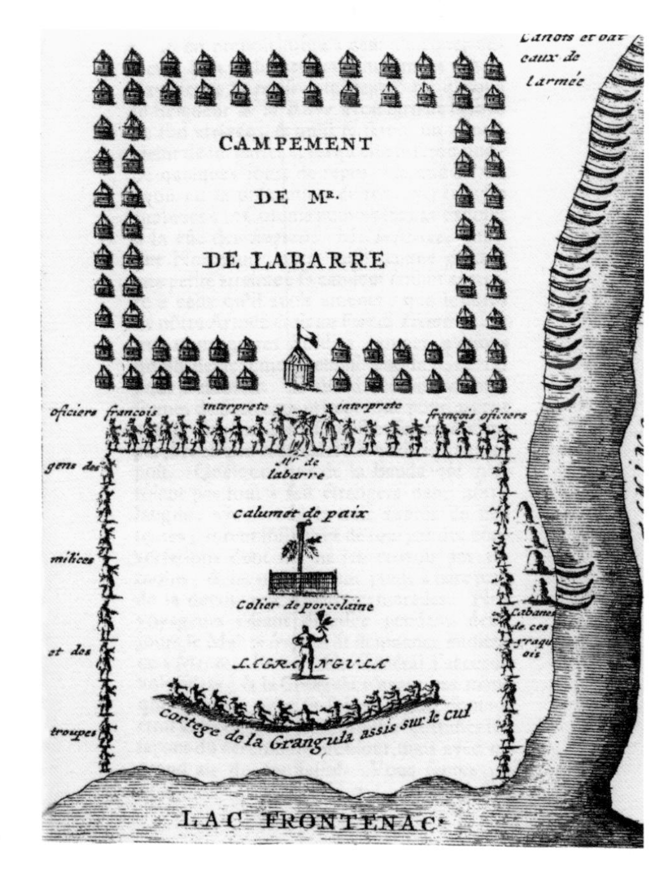

This entirely schematic drawing of the camp of La Barre's expedition on the southeast shore of Lake Ontario ("Lac Frontenac") in August 1684 shows, at top, the French camp. At the center of the row of figures below it, "M. De Labarre" is flanked by interpreters and French officers. Below him is a symbol of the peace-pipe (*calumet*), the figure of a chief ("Le Grangula"), and then his entourage of Iroquois chiefs sitting in an arc. Lines of militiamen and soldiers are shown on each side of the meeting-ground, and on the shore at the right canoes are drawn up. (Print after La Hontan's 1705 Amsterdam edition of his travels; author's photo)

Iroquois from taking the warpath by exercising his diplomatic talents. The following year it became clear that his successor lacked his abilities in this regard.

Canadian fur traders reported that friendly First Nations in the Illinois country had been decimated by the Iroquois, and there were rumors that once the latter had eliminated their rivals they planned to attack the French settlements. According to Canadians, the Iroquois were encouraged in this by officials and merchants in New England and New York. By the summer of 1683, Iroquois warriors were being seen closer to French settlements, and there were occasional bloody incidents; in practice, the peace treaty of 1668 was now a dead letter.

Unable to contain the situation, La Barre urgently appealed to Versailles for troops from France, and in November 1683 three companies of *Compagnies franches de la Marine* (Independent Naval Companies) arrived in Quebec. Now that he had 150 regular soldiers, La Barre decided on a show of force to deter the Iroquois. In July 1684 he also mustered some 700 Canadian militiamen and about 300–400 allied warriors; by August they reached Fort Frontenac, where they were joined by hundreds more warriors from western First Nations. In a sizeable fleet of boats and canoes, this force proceeded to the southeast shore of Lake Ontario and established a camp near the site of the later British Fort Oswego in upstate New York. La Barre's tactics were unimaginatively European, and his progress was watched every step of the way by unseen Iroquois. When he eventually invited Iroquois chiefs to meet him they took their time, while large numbers of their warriors were gathering in the area. In the French camp a rumor spread that if La Barre advanced further and attacked,

A

RAID TO HUDSON'S BAY, 1686

(1) Soldier, *Compagnies franches de la Marine*, winter

During large-scale summer expeditions, such as those led against the Iroquois by La Barre in 1684 and Denonville in 1687, the regular soldiers of the *Compagnies franches de la Marine* wore their European-issue regulation uniform (orders of July 1687 even mentioned that they had to clean their shoes, and not neglect to shave). For the 1686 winter expedition to Hudson's Bay, each regular soldier received a Canadian *capot* of blue wool cloth, which was decorated with "lace" (tape) edging (probably yellow or false-gold metallic); a red cloth shirt for cold weather, and two other shirts probably of linen; two pairs of stockings, or *mitasses* leggings in imitation of First Nations clothing, and a pair of cloth drawers; a pair of French shoes, two pairs of moccasins; and a flapped cloth cap of a style called *tapabord*. This soldier of the *Compagnies franches* has standard military equipment: a buff leather waist belt with Y-straps forming a sword-frog on the left hip, here with a tomahawk substituted for the regulation sword, and a sheathed plug bayonet attached to both the belt and the frog; a slung *gibicière* or *fourniment* bullet or cartridge pouch with the French royal arms embossed on the deep flap; and a pear-shaped flask for a pound of powder, made of leather-covered wood with a brass nozzle (officially for attachment below the pouch flap, it seems often to have been carried slung separately, which would make it quicker to use). Although flintlock muskets were widely used in Canada in the late 17th century, prior to 1690 the Navy Ministry's procurement of such weapons was somewhat haphazard; we have chosen to illustrate the weapon ordered in that year from the Tulle factory, with a 119mm (46.8in) barrel of 16mm caliber.

(2) Canadian militia volunteer, winter

For the 1686 operation each Canadian volunteer also received a cloth *capot* (but without lace trim), three linen shirts, a pair of *mitasses*, two handkerchiefs, two combs, a pair of French shoes, two pairs of moccasins, and a *tapabord* cap. Other items such as breeches and *mitasses* had to be provided by the individual. Like the snowshoes, mittens and scarves were essential in winter and early spring. This Canadian sports a waist sash, an Indigenous or homemade bullet bag, and a powder horn. His personally acquired flintlock musket, here in its protective bag, probably has a 121.8cm (45in) barrel of 14mm caliber. (AC, C11A, 8; Pierre, Chevalier de Troyes, *Journal de l'expédition du chevalier de Troyes à la Baie d'Hudson en 1686* (Ivanohé Caron, ed; Beauceville; L'Éclaireur, 1918))

(3) Assault on Fort Hayes, June 21

For the assault on Fort Hayes at Moose Factory, Hudson's Bay, some of Capt de Troyes' raiders broke down the gate with a log battering-ram fashioned on the spot, while others climbed over the 18ft (5.84m) stockade and jumped down inside. The use of battering-rams on surprise raids was occasionally repeated subsequently. Even this far north the June weather would have been relatively mild, and while some raiders might have retained their *capots* others would doubtless have fought in their shirtsleeves.

3
1
2

This expeditionary party in canoes could date from any time in the 17th or 18th centuries. As soon as rivers and lakes became navigable each spring, canoes were used for the fur trade, exploration and military raids; note too the priest – Jesuit missionaries were active in the wilderness, and sometimes served as chaplains for large raiding parties.

Handling birchbark canoes took skilled practice, but they were light enough to be unloaded and carried along *portage* trails bypassing rapids or linking rivers and lakes. By far the swiftest means to travel any distance, they gave access to North America's whole network of great rivers. From the St Lawrence, French explorers discovered the Ohio, the Illinois and the Mississippi, and claimed the territory along them as part of New France, right down to the Gulf of Mexico. (Print after Edmond J. Massicotte; private collection, author's photo)

hundreds of Anglo-Americans from New York led by Governor Thomas Dongan would join the Iroquois.

Since the camp was on swampy ground, fever broke out, and a food shortage also became evident – if La Barre had thought that his army could live off the land in the European style (which seems likely), he now learned the hard facts of life in America's wilderness. Iroquois chiefs finally appeared and, on September 5, negotiations opened. By then La Barre had a major epidemic in his camp, where some men were also close to starvation; with thousands of Iroquois rumored to be lurking nearby, it was time to retreat. The Iroquois chiefs made no real concessions apart from a promise (never kept) to pay for some damages, and with this paltry result the expedition returned to Canada. Not only was French prestige much reduced, but many men died from fever on the way back, and about 80 even after they had reached Montreal.

Following this failure, La Barre was recalled in 1685 and replaced by Jacques-René de Brisay, Marquis de Denonville (1637–1710), who landed at Quebec city on August 1. He was a brigadier-general who had commanded the La Reine Dragoon Regiment in Germany, but he lacked experience either as an army commander or as a territorial governor. Like his predecessor, Denonville had to face the Iroquois menace, but also other problems threatening the fur trade that was Canada's economic lifeblood. Since 1670, Britain had granted fur-trading rights to the Hudson's Bay Company, which had since installed several fortified trading posts on the shores of the Bay. Fur-traders in Canada had been granted the same rights on the Bay by the French government, in territory that was held to belong to France on the strength of previous exploration, but these had been usurped by the British traders. In 1684, although Britain and France were at peace, the Canadian trading fort on the Bay had been taken, razed, rebuilt, and armed with artillery by the Hudson's Bay Company.

A NEW TACTICAL DOCTRINE

In early 1686, Governor Denonville agreed with New France's merchants that the British forts on the Bay should be taken or destroyed, but how to actually achieve this was another matter. Most of the Company forts were built on the shores of James Bay, the southeastern extension of Hudson's Bay. Up to that time, French exploration and trade in the Bay had been carried out by ship. However, a number of Canadian *coureurs-des-bois* traders had ventured north into the vast area between Montreal and the Bay using canoes. Traders from New France did not sit in forts waiting for Indigenous customers to arrive; for decades, many had been venturing far into the wilderness to seek them out. By the 1670s, an unknown but certainly sizeable number of Canadians had enough experience to travel and prosper in the wilderness, providing the logistic knowhow for exploration beyond the Great Lakes.

By this point, the three sons of the aggressive merchant Charles Le Moyne had reached manhood. Two of them (Pierre and Paul) had been educated in France as junior naval officers, and they all had definite ideas about how to fight in North America. To them – as to their father, and other leading settler families such as the Hertels – the key lay in a combination of First Nations and European military practices.

By the end of 1685 the 19 young officers of the *Compagnies franches* already sent to Canada had realized that almost everything they had been taught regarding warfare in Europe was irrelevant in New France. In eastern and central North America, the distances between settlements were immense; nature was overwhelming, with endless forests and mighty rivers, and there were virtually no practical routes for military movements other than waterways. A large force could not march through such a wilderness: there were no roads, and nowhere to obtain food or take shelter on the way. It was all but impossible to move even light field artillery without slow and exhausting efforts, and cavalry was useless.

Obviously, the officers from France must have discussed this new environment with young Canadian gentlemen of the settler population. The Frenchmen initially deplored the "savage" Indigenous tactics of rushing out from hiding to kill or kidnap unsuspecting opponents or civilians. Their gentlemanly instincts rebelled against taking cover to shoot unseen at the enemy, and then running away, hiding anew, and doing it again. Their culture required them to stand and fight bravely face-to-face, with bayonets fixed and colors flying, to the sound of fifes, drums and artillery. European soldiers were drilled in body and mind to be stoic and steady in the line of battle, and to obey "articles of war" that could send a man to the gallows for breaches of discipline. But the primary type of offensive action among the First Nations was the ambush – and indeed, warriors might not agree even to this if they felt the odds were against them. They were basically independent individuals, who had to be convinced by, and confident in, their war chiefs before any action was undertaken. Yet there could be no doubt that the Indigenous warriors were very brave, in their

Pierre Le Moyne d'Iberville (1661–1706), one of the sons of the leading settler and trader Charles Le Moyne, is considered to have been New France's greatest soldier. As redoubtable on the deck of a warship as he was in the wilderness, he led in many actions on land and sea, from Hudson's Bay to the West Indies. He is also credited with one of his brothers, Bienville, with establishing the first French settlement in Louisiana. He finally died of yellow fever in Havana in 1706, after raiding the British Leeward Islands. (Print after portrait; private collection, author's photo)

While this period print actually represents D'Iberville's capture of Fort Nelson on Hudson's Bay in 1694, the general aspect of the fort was much the same as the three forts at James Bay taken by Capt de Troyes' 1686 expedition, in which D'Iberville also served. (Detail from print after Bacqueville de la Potherie; courtesy Library and Archives Canada, C1113194)

way, and were outstandingly fit and knowledgeable woodsmen who moved fast over great distances. Most of all, their way of fighting had the effect of keeping European foes apprehensive – even terrified, at times – and nearly always on the defensive.

Once considerations of European "gallantry" and Christian humanity were laid aside, a cold-blooded analysis of the results of such ways of fighting could only lead French officers to the conclusion that, in the environment of New France, "parade-ground" maneuvers by lines of soldiers firing volleys (initially, covered by pikemen), were not only ineffective but potentially disastrous. The regulars had already shown themselves quite inadequate when pursuing Indigenous enemies; their only strength lay in garrisoning forts with superior firepower, while hopefully avoiding being ambushed when outside them.

One officer who arrived in August 1685 was the young Capt Pierre, Chevalier de Troyes (16??–88), who soon impressed Denonville as "the most intelligent and the most capable of our commanders ... wise, sensible, and full of good will." Pierre de Troyes obviously learned a great deal from the Le Moyne brothers in particular. Together the young French Navy and Canadian Militia officers came up with a revolutionary proposal for solving the problem of the British presence on Hudson's Bay: a military expedition *overland* from Montreal to James Bay – a distance of at least 745 miles (1,200km), over which no route had yet been established. The route suggested was up the Ottawa River, but instead of taking the Madawaska River west to Lake Huron like most fur traders, it would continue north on the Ottawa River, cross Lake Témiscamingue, continue via *portages* and small rivers to Lake Abitibi, and thence to James Bay down the Abitibi River.

The French had available to them exemplars of how Europeans could achieve such a journey: the wilderness-loving *coureurs-des-bois* and *voyageurs* who maintained the vital fur trade. These Canadians had friendly relations with the First Nations that were their trading partners, and were familiar with their lifestyles; indeed, some Canadians had adopted elements of the Indigenous way of life in order to enjoy more personal freedom than was afforded in the settlements (for instance, nearly every Canadian practiced hunting and fishing, forbidden to most people in Old France). Alongside these locals, after two years in New France some of the French-born officers and soldiers were also gradually becoming more experienced and effective in the wilderness.

The first organized raid, 1686

Its proposers convinced Governor Denonville that such an expedition was possible. On February 12, 1686, he appointed Capt de Troyes to command the raid, with the Canadians Jacques Le Moyne de Sainte-Hélène as first lieutenant, Pierre Le Moyne d'Iberville as second lieutenant, Paul Le Moyne de Maricourt as *major*, Zacharie Robutel, Sieur de La Noue as *aide-major*, the Jesuit Father Silvy as chaplain, and Pierre Allemand as commissioner of supplies, doubling as naval pilot in case English ships were taken in the Bay. The rankers were picked men: 30 volunteer soldiers from the *Compangnies franches*, including a sergeant and a surgeon, and 65 trained Canadian militiamen who were experienced travelers. For such a trek into the barren north in winter, all members of the party had to be both strong-minded and in excellent physical condition.

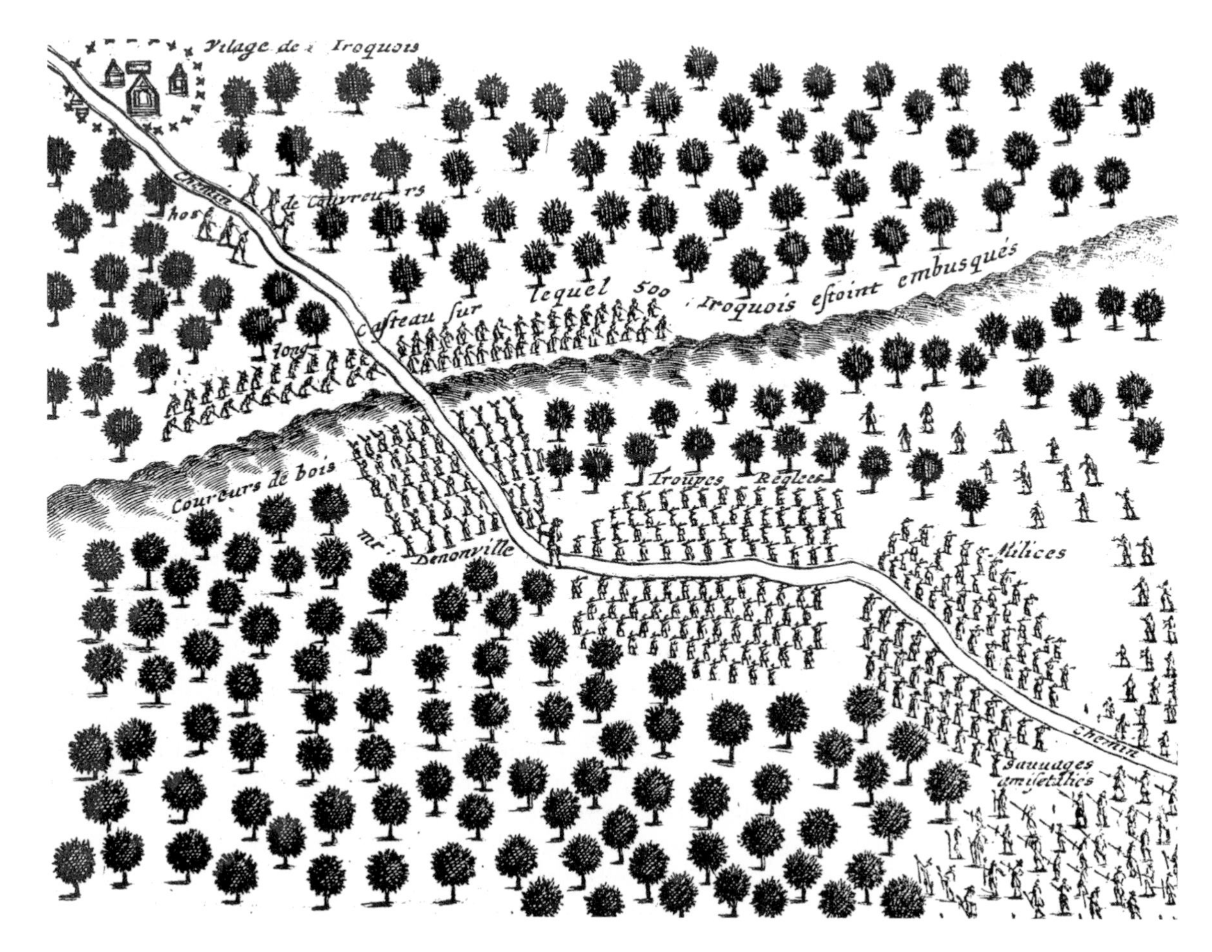

Schematic drawing of Denonville's engagement with Seneca warriors during his expedition of August 1687. At top left, the Iroquois village; center left, "*500 Iroquois*" concealed along a ridge. The first French unit approaching them are "*coureurs-des-bois*" of the Canadian militia, shown in ranked formation. Denonville is shown behind them on the trail, ahead of two regular units of the *Compagnies franches de la Marine*; then two more units of militiamen, some hooking forward to scout and skirmish on the right flank; and finally, a crescent of allied "savages." (Print after La Hontan's 1705 Amsterdam edition of his travels; author's photo)

Equipment of February 1686 raid to Hudson's Bay (see AC, C11A, 8)

The list includes 37 canoes, with toboggans to drag them "over the ice," and more toboggans for other supplies. Some 74 small and large brass cooking pots, 230 axes of various types, 60 sulfured torches, 50 pairs of snowshoes, 100 shovels, and quantities of black powder, lead and flints were also taken. The weapons included 150 flintlock muskets with their cloth bags, 100 plug bayonets, 50 pistols, 60 swords or sabers, 50 grenades, and two rifled muskets (presumably for the best marksmen), and each militiaman was also issued two knives. The rations included salt pork, ham, sea biscuits, rice, dried corn and pease, salt, pepper, cloves, brandy and tobacco. European uniforms were out of the question for a wilderness expedition in winter, and the soldiers received a special issue of Canadian-style clothing (see Plate A) – seemingly for the first time.

This operation needed faultless planning, and in a sense the preparations were comparable to those for a ship's crew going to sea. The essential aspect was that the authorities had to provide adequate logistics; long military expeditions needed to be able to transport a lot of supplies and equipment if they were to reach their objective and return successfully. Everything that would be needed – from food and drink for three months, to tools for repairing canoes and snowshoes – had to be taken along by the raiding party (see panel). Never before had such a raiding expedition had been so thoroughly organized, and it provided a basic model for others by French and Canadian personnel for decades to come – though details would naturally vary, and uniformity in clothing does not seem to have been as important thereafter.

In Canada, even in the south before the end of the 20th century, ice would still cover rivers and lakes until spring thaws usually occurred gradually from late March. In the event, when the expedition marched out of Montreal on March 30, 1686, it found the ice unstable due to an early thaw, and this slowed progress. In the weeks that followed the raiders would experience icy rain, or days of very cold weather; ice coming down the Ottawa River damaged some of the canoes, so men often had to walk along the river's edge, sometimes up to their chests in icy water. For *portages* to bypass the river's rapids everything had to be unloaded and carried overland; the largest rapids, in the area of present-day Ottawa/Gatineau, were reached in late April. D'Iberville was nearly drowned, like one of his companions, when their canoe overturned in a cataract. As it grew warmer the rivers were more navigable, but there were still countless tiring *portages*, and another danger, a forest fire, was only narrowly avoided.

By May, Capt de Troyes had found that rigid discipline did not work for independent-minded Canadians as it did for his French soldiers, but fortunately he took Father Silvy's advice to soften his manner. On May 18, the expedition reached the farthest French trading post above Montreal, at Lake Témiscamingue. From there, they paddled across the lake and eventually reached Lake Abitibi. Finally, on June 20, after some 85 days' travel, the British fort at Moose Factory on the shore of James Bay came in sight. The party stayed quietly under cover while Capt de Troyes discreetly surveyed the objective.

The taking of Forts Hayes, Rupert, and Albany

Fort Hayes was made of squared timber with walls 18ft high (5.84m), with a robust timber gate reinforced with iron straps. It had four bastions, each with four 2-pounder light cannon. Inside was a large three-story redoubt doubling as quarters, which mounted three more 2-pdrs and a brass 8-pounder. This and other structures accommodated 18 men.

A Canadian volunteer scouting in winter. Raiders always put out scouts ahead, on the flanks, and following the main party of a large expedition. If they spotted something, they would stealthily rejoin the main group to warn them, so that they could take cover, remaining silent and motionless to preserve the vital element of surprise. (Print after Edmond J. Massicotte; private collection, author's photo)

Capt de Troyes resolved to attack as soon as possible, while their presence was still undetected. There were no sentries posted, and Sainte-Hélène even sneaked up to some cannon muzzles and inserting his ramrod to see if they were loaded. Dogs inside the fort were barking occasionally – they had smelled or heard something – but their masters took no notice; it was unimaginable to them that a large French raiding party was just outside.

In the early morning of June 21, the raiders divided into three detachments and approached the fort. Still undetected, two detachments climbed up the wall and, on a signal from Capt de Troyes, Sainte-Hélène and his brothers jumped into the fort sword in hand. Meanwhile, the other detachment started battering the gate with a log made into a rudimentary ram, while others opened fire. The startled garrison woke up and, still in their nightshirts, opened fire from windows; Troyes' interpreter soon told him that some of the English traders were calling for quarter. But the interpreter was spurned by an English gunner, who was trying to point a cannon – until killed by a shot in the head, possibly by the noted marksman Sainte-Hélène. Most of the garrison fled into the redoubt, followed by D'Iberville who, initially alone, slashed with his sword and fired his pistol; when other raiders joined him, the garrison surrendered. The fighting had lasted about half an hour. It was the benchmark for the classic surprise raid in North America, to be repeated in countless actions for many decades to come.

Leaving part of his force at Fort Hayes with the prisoners, Troyes led the Le Moyne brothers and 60 men about 124 miles (200km) to Fort Rupert, where they found a Hudson's Bay Company ship at anchor. On July 3, in a simultaneous dawn double attack, both fort and ship were captured. Approaching silently in canoes, D'Iberville with 13 men boarded the ship and took it after he shot a sentry and cut down a sailor. Meanwhile his brother Sainte-Hélène burst into the fort, which soon surrendered. There were about

30 prisoners (including a woman wounded when a stove burst after one of the raiders threw a grenade down the redoubt's chimney). After destroying Rupert House, the expedition regrouped at Moose Factory before setting out to capture Fort Albany about 100 miles (160km) to the northwest.

This time they also had the captured ship with artillery on board. Once in view of the target the raiders landed, and since there was no element of surprise Capt de Troyes changed his tactics. He had a covered battery built on land, and Pierre Allemand even managed to produce homemade shells. On July 26, after a rather vague response to a surrender demand, the raiders fired some 140 shots within an hour, to which the fort's guns answered only weakly. The bombardment drove the garrison into the cellar of the redoubt, before the commander capitulated with about 30 men and two women. The raid's total booty came to about 200,000 *livres*-worth of furs. [2]

In some triumph, the young French and Canadian officers returned to Canada, having put their theories to the test with outstanding success. It might be argued that the English forts had no regular garrisons, but Capt de Troyes himself had only 30 regular soldiers. Everyone knew that

2 The forts on the Bay were later retaken by the English, and subsequently captured again by the French, until the 1713 Treaty of Utrecht finally conceded Hudson's Bay to Britain.

B

CANADIAN MILITIA, EARLY–MID 18th CENTURY

Clothing and equipment was usually the volunteer's own; even if some garments were issued, they were not necessarily "uniform" (see detailed descriptions in body text, "Material culture: Canadian dress"). This plate simply reconstructs some typical examples of "wilderness" dress; there were few notable changes between the late 17th and mid-18th centuries, apart from occasionally to gentlemen's hairstyles, and the belated acquisition of successive issues of some French Navy and Army equipment.

(1) Militia officer, spring–autumn

Apart from the *tapabord* (see Plate A), the usual wool caps were stocking- or "nightcap"-shaped, in this case a type with fur trim. Red caps may have been associated more with Quebec, white with Trois-Rivières and blue with Montreal, but this was far from consistent. The roughly knee-length *capot* shown here is the most typical style for moderate weather, and in the early 18th century about half of them were probably blue. The double-breasted front was either fastened across to the upper right button, or left unbuttoned and gathered only by the waist sash. Pockets had no flaps; the cuffs might be this "boot" type, buttoned at the top, or might have a simple buttoned vent or flap as **(B2)**. Like a European coat, the *capot* was tailored to the waist; it had a deep central rear vent, might have rear pleats from hip buttons as **(B2)**, and always had a pointed hood. Militia officers' status was indicated by a crescent-shaped gilded gorget suspended at the throat, which might bear engraved royal arms and trophies, or later an applied silver badge. The quality of the clothing worn under the coat depended upon an individual's means; this officer has a pair of fine plush knee breeches, but over his white stockings he chooses to wear knee-length Indigenous boot-moccasins. In the wilderness he does not carry his sword; his weapons are a Tulle musket with the 1716 modification that added "grenadier" sling attachments, and a Navy 1716 flintlock pistol. He has a slung horn-and-brass powder flask of the type used from *c.*1700 until the 1750s, and carries his other necessities in an Indigenous "bandolier bag" decorated with quillwork.

(2) Militiaman, winter

This is another common cap, turned up at the bottom to show a band of the lining color. The hair might be worn either in a wrapped queue, "clubbed," or loose. His *capot* might be of longer winter length than this, reaching to low on the calf. In the early 18th century only some 6 percent seem to have been made in brown cloth, though this rose to about 25 percent from the 1740s. Below wool cloth breeches, which might be lined with soft leather for winter, he would wear knit stockings, and his blanket-cloth *mitasses* are decorated at the edges with tape in a contrasting color – red and blue seem to have been common. Hardly visible on his feet are ankle-length gray cloth winter *nippes* worn inside high-flapped deerskin moccasins. Sashes were of a range of solid colors and served the purpose of a waist belt. The felling axe is military issue.

(3) *Coureur-des-bois*, hot weather

In summer a lighter stocking cap might be worn, but equally a simple bandana. Canadians who mingled with the First Nations might copy their practice of tattooing. The shirt alone was the basic summer garment, and is worn here only with the belt-supported breechclout and *mitasses*, as used by the First Nations. *Mitasses* might be of fringed deerskin as Plate A2, but the type illustrated here, showing stripes near the upper edge, was made from a trade blanket. Again like the warriors, Canadians might carry as many as three knives – from the neck, in the sash, and from a knee-garter. The musket is a typical hunting type imported commercially. (Francis Back & René Chartrand, "Canadian Militia 1750–1760," in *Military Collector & Historian: Journal of the Company of Military Historians*, Vol. XXXVI, No. 1, Spring 1984; Francis Back, "S'habiller à la canadienne," in *Cap-aux-Diamants: la revue d'histoire du Québec*, No. 24, 1991; Steve Delisle, *The Equipment of New France Militia 1740–1760* (Bel Air, MD; Kebec Liber Ata, 1999))

1
2
3

the expedition could never had succeeded without the Canadian militiamen, whose wilderness experience was crucial. However, New France was soon reminded that another important factor was still missing before this type of warfare could become truly formidable: harnessing the First Nations to the program.

Denonville's Seneca campaign, 1687

In the meantime, small but violent incidents continued, with settlers being ambushed, killed and scalped, or disappearing forever in the hands of the Iroquois. French diplomatic relations were worsening with both the Iroquois confederacy and the Anglo-American colonies. In 1686, La Hontan notes that most of the regular troops in Canada were posted defensively in the Montreal area, but once Governor Denonville received strong reinforcements of *Compagnies franches* from France in June 1687, he assembled a field force. After issuing marching orders (specifying that soldiers were to keep their uniforms neat and to be clean shaven, according to Baugy's journal), he now went on the offensive, against the Seneca nation of the Iroquois confederacy.

His little army boarded some 200 flat-bottomed *bateaux*, (including two for artillery) and 200 canoes for the voyage to Fort Frontenac. There, Denonville committed a most reprehensible act. He had previously invited many Iroquois chiefs and warriors to a grand banquet at the fort. It was in fact a ruse to capture them just before his arrival, and about a hundred were taken, put in chains and eventually jailed in Quebec city. Adding insult to injury, he then chose to apply French law rigidly, and shipped 36 of them back to Marseille to pull oars as convicts in the French Navy's Mediterranean galley fleet. Denonville's treachery was long remembered by the Iroquois.

A much later artist's impression of the Iroquois night attack on the village of Lachine, August 1689. Though the losses were much exaggerated at the time, this event was indeed the bloodiest of its kind in the history of New France. The reaction was to have considerable consequences on how warfare was carried out in North America for decades to come. (Print in *Histoire du Canada*, 1912; author's photo)

From Fort Frontenac, Denonville continued to the southeast shore of Lake Ontario, landing in mid-July 1687 with 843 soldiers of the *Compagnies franches*, 804 militiamen, and 353 allied warriors. Encountering no opposition, they moved inland to destroy the Senecas' towns; to avoid ambushes, Denonville marched with advance and rear guards and put out scouts on each side of the column. When they neared the first town, some 300–500 Senecas were spotted on a ridge and, in European style, the troops formed into battalions and prepared to charge, but were forestalled by a rush of warriors. Unnerved by the war cries, some soldiers and militiamen broke ranks, but La Barre immediately ordered the drums beaten to reform the line. This succeeded, and, after firing some volleys, the French-led force charged the Senecas. After a short but fierce fight the overwhelmed Senecas broke and ran (according to the French – but Colden reports that according to what Anglo-Americans learned from their allies, they retreated in good order). A report in the November 1687 *Mercure Galant* put Seneca losses at 24 killed and over 60 wounded, while Denonville lost an officer, four Frenchmen, and four warriors killed and 14 wounded. (The Anglo-Americans were told that about 100 Frenchmen and 10 allied warriors were killed, against 40 Seneca dead. Such competing claims are impossible to confirm.)

The Senecas abandoned their homes and vanished into the wilderness, while the French burned their towns and crops. The damage suffered by the Senecas was apparently not too grave: apprehensive of a counterattack, Denonville had withdrawn before finding many of their hidden food caches. All in all, it was hardly a French triumph; the regular troops had set rather a lackluster example, while some Canadian militiamen had wavered when sent into battle in a ranked formation rather than as skirmishers.

Nevertheless, satisfied that he had struck a hard blow, Denonville detached some troops to build a fort at Niagara before returning to Montreal, where he waited for the Iroquois chiefs to come in and sue for peace. Instead, while making vague peace overtures, all the Iroquois nations vowed revenge, planned raids, and sought encouragement from the Anglo-American colonies. Eventually Denonville realized one of his mistakes and asked that the Iroquois condemned to the galleys be sent back, but few were.

Overall, Denonville's expedition had solved nothing: the Iroquois remained just as threatening as ever and mounted several small raids. In the fall of 1687 two soldiers and four inhabitants were ambushed and killed on the western end of the island of Montreal, while several settlers were kidnapped near Chambly. Disease broke out among isolated garrisons, leading to fears that outposts would become untenable; sure enough, during summer 1688 Denonville chose to withdraw the now very sickly garrison from the new fort at Niagara, and the following year that of Fort Frontenac – thus abandoning Lake Ontario.

Meanwhile, the "Glorious Revolution" in England had deposed King James II, who had been well disposed towards France, and installed in his place William of Orange, the Dutch archrival of Louis XIV, as its King William III. The new British king decided to recognize the Iroquois as allied subjects who would enjoy his protection. In August 1688, Sir Edmund Andros, governor of New England, informed Denonville of the Iroquois' new status; he added that he would ensure they did no harm to the French, but few believed this was either credible or possible.

By now French influence and trade on lakes Ontario and Erie had all but vanished, and Frontenac's diplomatic achievements were in ruins: the allied First Nations were starting to doubt the power of their current French *Onontio*. Despite successive deployments to New France of about 30 companies totaling some 1,500 French Navy regulars since 1683, the fears of many Canadians seemed justified when news came that Britain had declared war on France in May 1689 (in the War of the Grand Alliance, 1689–97, known in America as "King William's War"). Despite the

C

COMPAGNIES FRANCHES, EARLY–MID 18th CENTURY

(1) Sergeant, garrison dress, *c.*1720s

By 1689 there were 28 Independent Naval Companies in New France, though in 1699 the establishment of a company was reduced from 50 to 30 men, with a total establishment of 84 officers and 840 sergeants and privates. This figure reconstructs a uniform worn in Canada; those worn in Acadia and at Placentia in *c.* 1701-16 had notable differences – e.g. sergeants had blue coats.

The tricorn hat was edged with false-gold lace for soldiers and gold for sergeants. Over the white shirt and neck-cloth all ranks wore a long-sleeved, single-breasted, collarless *veste* cut nearly as long as the uniform coat. The collarless, single-breasted *justaucorps* uniform coat was of gray-white cloth, this *gris-blanc* shade varying considerably. Lined with blue, the coat was normally worn open revealing the *veste*. Before 1701, 60 brass coat buttons were provided; in *c.* 1701-16, 24 white metal; and from *c.* 1716 on, 36 brass. The coat had a deep central vent at the rear and, flanking this, a number of pleats from rear hip buttons; these latter were the upper of three buttons spaced down side vents that concealed functioning pockets. The pocket flaps on the front were false, which allowed fanciful placing of the five buttons, and the coat had a single left shoulder strap of coat-cloth to secure the sling of the original bullet pouch. The soldier's blue *en botte* cuffs had three or four buttons at the top and plain buttonholes; the sergeant's, a top edging and (*c.*1716–50) buttonhole "loops" of gold lace. The *veste*, knee breeches and stockings were gray-white until *c.* 1716-18 and blue thereafter, and the high-tongued shoes black with a brass buckle. This sergeant's weapons are a straight sword with a gilded brass hilt (emerging through side and rear vents of his coat), and the 1714 halberd for Naval troops.

A 1747 account by Walter Butler mentioned a young French officer "dressed in blue with a broad gold lace," possibly his laced uniform *veste*; this garment is likely to have been worn instead of a coat by all ranks during summer on the frontier. (Michel Petard, "L'Homme de 1736: Le Fusilier au début de la Guerre de Succession d'Autriche," in *Uniformes* 55, May–June 1980; Michel Petard, "L'Homme de 1751: Les compagnies franches de la Marine," in *Uniformes* 34, November–December 1976; René Chartrand, *French Military Arms and Armor in America 1503–1783* (Mowbray, Woonsocket RI; 2016))

(2) Soldier, winter field dress, mid-1690s

By the time of Frontenac's 1696 summer expedition it is not certain how the regulars were dressed, but a mixture of both European (for the majority) and Canadian styles is probable. There was a short-lived experiment in 1694–96 to issue soldiers in Canada with these *capots* of gray-white serge "garnished with blue serge [from] Aumale and cuffs and buttons" (F1A, 8). Supplies of the European uniform were periodically sent up to small western forts until about 1732, when Intendant Gilles Hocquart ended this expensive practice. Thereafter, soldiers posted to such outposts left Montreal wearing their regulation dress but would then procure replacement clothing from the fort's trade store, keeping their issue uniform for formal occasions, and wearing more comfortable and practical alternatives for everyday service. These were not always from trade stores, however, and references mention soldiers' *capots d'ordonnance* ("regulation *capots*") made from old uniform coats, which again seems to suggest gray-white with blue cuffs.

Into the early 18th century equipment consisted of the *gibicière* pouch slung across from the left shoulder with an attached or separate powder flask and priming flask, and a buff sword belt at the waist, the sword usually being replaced with a tomahawk. This soldier wears the less common of two types of canvas knapsack with canvas or leather straps; this was shaped as a bag, with the top gathered and tied, and our man has hitched to it a small cooking cauldron or "kettle."

(3) Soldier, summer field dress, early 1740s

The fatigue caps were made from worn-out uniforms; those in Canada were probably gray-white with a blue turn-up, or all blue, and may have sported false-gold edging and a lily badge in front (uniformity was not a priority in the wilderness). The exact form of the early *bonnet de police* is unclear, but scholars suggest that at least by the 18th century it was made *à la dragonne*, with a long tasseled bag as illustrated. The shortened *capot* for warm seasons is worn over the shirt and Indigenous-style breechclout and *mitasses*.

Early in the 18th century the *gibicière* was replaced with the *gargoussier* cartridge box (holding nine rounds in a drilled, slightly curved wooden block) worn on the right front of the waist belt. From about 1715 to the late 1740s its leather flap was edged with a white saw-tooth border and bore a central white anchor, this being replaced thereafter with a plain flap stamped with the royal arms. The slightly curved, flattened powder flask issued throughout the first half of the 18th century was made of molded horn with brass fittings, and hung from its own narrow buff strap.

The waist belt now had a double frog for bayonet and sword or tomahawk; from 1722 to the early 1750s the 18in (45.7cm) bayonet had a long shank between socket and blade. The musket shown is the Navy model ordered in 1734, with a shorter 42in (106.7cm) barrel and a single barrel-band for a forward sling-ring on the left side. The knapsack is the more popular of the two types: a rectangular canvas bag slung on a single diagonal canvas or leather strap from right shoulder to left hip, its doubled top being folded down outside and secured by a cord around the pack.

1
2
3

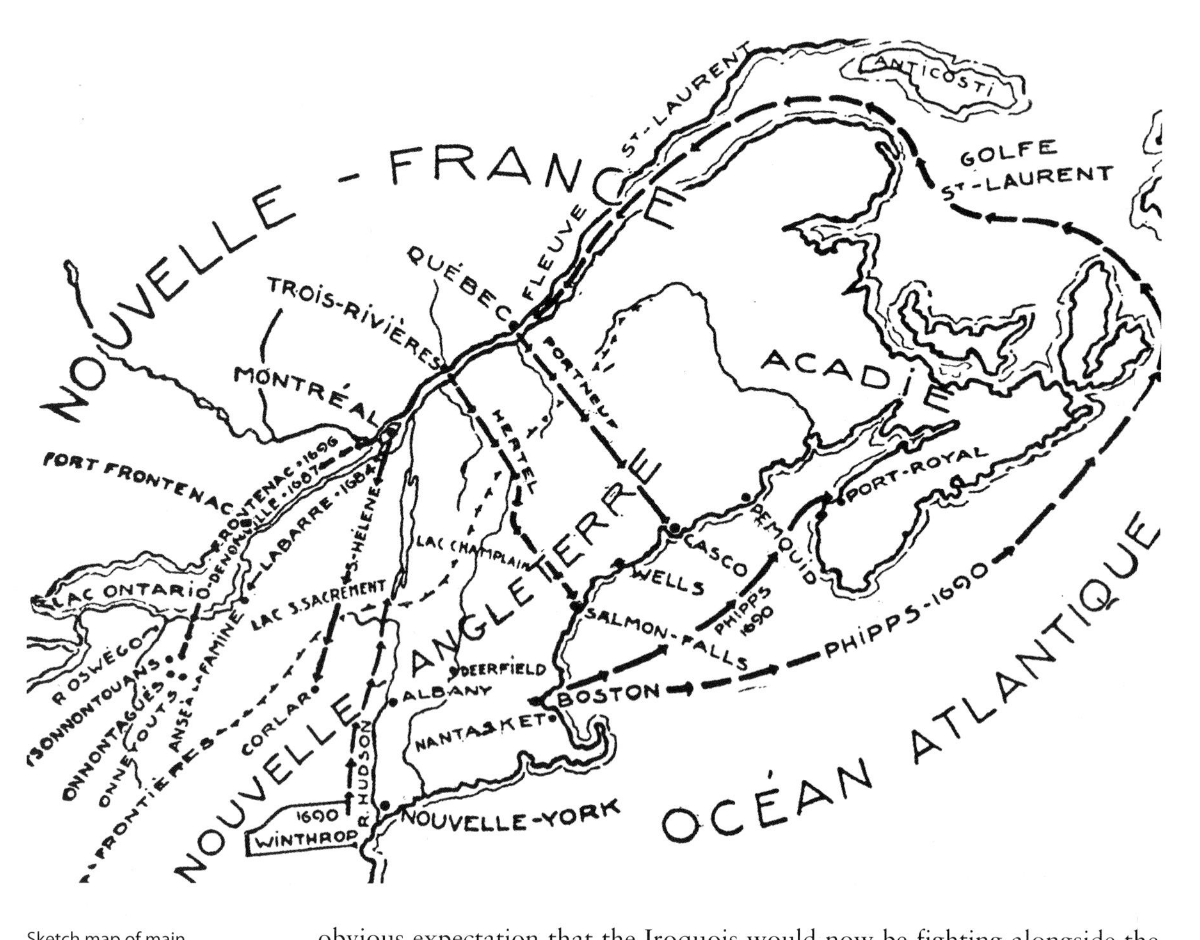

Sketch map of main expeditions and raids, 1684–1696. The first were by La Barre (1684) and Denonville (1687) down into the Iroquois country east and south of Lake Ontario. Then came the three French raids (1690) from Montreal on "Corlar" (Schenectady), from Trois-Rivières on Salmon Falls, and from Quebec on Casco (Falmouth). The same year saw Phipp's [sic] capture of Port-Royal in Acadia (Nova Scotia), and unsuccessful siege of Quebec, and Winthrop's abortive march to Lake Champlain. Frontenac crossed south of Lake Ontario to attack the Iroquois nations (1696). During "Queen Anne's War" raids would reach Deerfield and Haverhill near Albany and Boston (1704 & 1708). (From *Histoire du Canada*, 1912; author's photo)

obvious expectation that the Iroquois would now be fighting alongside the Anglo-Americans, initially the confederacy remained relatively quiet; some in Canada even wondered if they might not actually wish to negotiate a separate peace.

"King William's War": Lachine, 1689

That delusion was destroyed on the night of August 4/5, 1689 at Lachine, a large village just west of Montreal. Allegedly as many as 1,200–1,500 Iroquois approached in canoes under cover of heavy rain and a hailstorm. Whatever the true numbers, they landed quietly, and surrounded most of the houses without waking the inhabitants. At a signal, war-cries rent the night, doors were battered down, and dazed and terrified men, women and children were killed or seized, while 56 of the 77 houses were set on fire. Once it seemed that Montreal itself would not be attacked, soldiers eventually came out of nearby forts to intervene, but far too late, and some were repulsed in skirmishes with Iroquois rearguards.

While some 250 villagers somehow managed to escape, about 24 were killed on the spot and some 42 made prisoners. However, these relatively modest figures were only carefully computed a century later by Désiré Girouard; on August 6, 1689, when news of what became notorious as the "Lachine Massacre" broke, it was as if a thunderbolt had struck New France. According to panic-stricken accounts, more than 200 people had been butchered, and as many as 120 prisoners had been cruelly burned alive. Stories of unprintable atrocities inflicted on some of the victims spread crippling fear and desperation throughout the colony.

RAID WARFARE

Frontenac's return

Meanwhile, in Versailles, the embattled Louis XIV had not totally forgotten New France. Clearly, Denonville had not produced the desired results, and while the king would not learn of the Lachine disaster until the late fall of 1689, as early as that spring he had understood the colony's need for a better governor. Called to an audience with the king, the Comte de Frontenac was told simply: "I am sending you back to Canada, where I expect you will serve me as well as you previously have. I ask you for no more." Frontenac was now 68 years old, but as fiery as ever. Other French plans delayed his departure, but on October 15, 1689 Frontenac arrived at Quebec city to be greeted by cheering crowds, bonfires, and cannon salutes. A traumatized population were looking to him as their savior.

It was essential to reassure the allied First Nations that their *Onontio* was back and meant business, and Frontenac must soon have conferred with François Hertel de La Fresnière, the "*commandant*" of allied First Nations who had been appointed by La Barre (in modern terms, this title meant a French chief adviser imbedded with the Indigenous peoples). Born in Trois-Rivières, Hertel had been a soldier in that town's garrison when only 15 years old, and, like Charles Le Moyne, had acquired exceptional knowledge of Indigenous languages and culture, in his case during a two-year captivity amongst the Iroquois from which he managed to escape.[3] Fascinated by the First Nations, Hertel became a valued interpreter, and volunteered for many parties to oppose Iroquois marauders. He understood that allied warriors were independent, unpredictable, and totally unsuited to European military discipline, but believed they could have a very positive effect if joined with organized war parties of French soldiers and Canadian militiamen drawing upon the practical lessons of the 1686 raid to Hudson's Bay.

Frontenac now found many of his officers promoting a radically new and different style of fighting, and eager to put their concepts to the test. To Frontenac and nearly everyone else in New France, the real culprits of Lachine were the Anglo-Americans, who had to be made to understand that they would suffer consequences for encouraging such outrages. Despite the huge disparity in numbers, this was not an impossible ambition. Massachusetts had 58,000 inhabitants of European origin, Connecticut some 22,000, New York 14,000, and Rhode Island 5,000, giving a total population of perhaps 100,000. By contrast, New France had about 12,000 souls. However, New France had the great advantage of a unified military command under its governor, more than 100 professional officers and up

3 Again like Le Moyne, François Hertel fathered several sons who inherited his belief in wilderness tactics. Zacharie-François (1665–1752), Jacques Hertel de Cournoyer (1667–1748), and Jean-Baptiste Hertel de Rouville (1668–1722) all became regular officers in the *Compagnies franches*, and took part in a number of raids.

There is no known period likeness of Louis de Bruade, Comte de Frontenac (1622–98), the most famous governor-general of New France, but this late 19th-century statue by Philippe Hébert at Quebec's National Assembly has become his image in countless publications. His determined expression as he points to the cannon recalls his defiance of the New England siege of Quebec city in October 1690. As important as his fiery energy was his understanding of the First Nations, whose negotiated assistance was crucial. Apart from more serious inducements, he often entertained their chiefs as guests at his table, where he might even offer them the rare novelty of ice cream in the colors of several flavors. (Private collection; author's photo)

This woodcut supposedly illustrating the plundering and burning of Schenectady on February 8, 1690 is not a historical document, but it does give a realistically stark idea of the terror inspired by such raids, especially when (as was usually the case) First Nations warriors formed part of the expeditions. (From John Russel's *A History of the United States of America*, 1814; private collection, author's photo)

to 1,500 regular soldiers, while the manpower pool of the well-organized Canadian Militia boasted a high proportion of men familiar with firearms and comfortable in the wilderness.

Schenectady, Salmon Falls, and Falmouth, 1690

By January 1690, Frontenac had endorsed the Canadians' opinions that First Nations-style raids with European leadership, participation and organization were the best way to strike back. The plan was ambitious: three simultaneous expeditions would leave Montreal, Trois-Rivières and Quebec to raid communities in New York and New England in winter, and this time (probably at Hertel's urging) allied warriors would join the essentially Canadian war parties. Relatively few regular soldiers apart from Canadian-born officers were then proficient in winter travel overland, but many Canadians with experience in the fur trade were.

The largest expedition left Montreal under the command of Le Moyne de Sainte-Hélène, with Le Moyne d'Iberville, D'Aillebout de Mantet, de Répentigny, de La Brosse and de Montigny leading 114 Canadians and 96 allied warriors. The party marched south on snowshoes through the winter forest, and were eventually told by the officers that their target was Albany in New York colony. The warriors protested that it was too strong and well-garrisoned to assault, but they agreed to attack nearby Schenectady, a small town said to supply arms to the Iroquois.

After a difficult trek through deep snow in bitter cold, the party were within sight of their target's stockade walls on the night of February 8. The high wind was raising clouds of snow; no sentries could be seen, and a gate was even partly ajar, so it was decided to attack at once. Five or six men went to each house in the sleeping township, and then raised a great war-whoop. (Copied by the Canadians from the warriors, this consisted of a yell made "while hitting their mouths several times ... for two purposes: to terrify a surprised enemy and also serve as a signal," according to Beauchêne.) The raiders rapidly broke down doors and attacked anyone who moved inside the darkened homes. Some tried to resist, and about 60 persons of both sexes and all ages were killed, before the place was set on fire. Only one Canadian and a warrior were killed in the attack, and late the next morning Le Moyne de Sainte-Hélène's party headed back to Canada with 27 prisoners and about 50 captured horses laden with booty.

Portrait copy by Henri Beau, believed to show François Hertel de la Fresnière (1642–1722), originally portrayed in *c.*1690. Born in Trois-Rivières into a leading settler family, François fought in his youth against the marauding Iroquois, who captured and adopted him in 1661. By the time he escaped two years later he had learned their language and war-culture, thereafter becoming an interpreter and volunteer participating in many actions and other events. In 1682 he was made "*commandant*" of the French-allied First Nations, and in 1690 he led the raid on Salmon Falls. Commissioned an officer in the regular troops the following year, he continued to render many services. In 1716, he was ennobled – a rare reward in Canada. However, François is not recorded as being a knight of the Order of Saint-Louis, so its cross here may identify the subject as his son Zacharie-François (1665–1752), who was knighted in 1744. (Courtesy Library and Archives Canada, C10605)

By then the alarm had been sounded. Militiamen from Albany and its surroundings, as well as Iroquois warriors, mustered to pursue the raiding party, which the wildest rumors put at anything up to 1,400 men. The pursuit was not very effective; the Albany militiamen were hampered by "Snow above Knee Deep," while Iroquois warriors, impressed by the attack, were wondering if their "castles" were also about to be targeted. Nevertheless, some 140 warriors followed the tracks of the raiders and captured 19 stragglers, who were later put to cruel deaths. The rest of the Schenectady raiders eventually reached Montreal with their prisoners and 16 horses, the others having been eaten on the way (DHNY, I).

François Hertel de la Fresnière led the smaller war party that marched out of Trois-Rivières on January 28, 1690. It consisted of 50 Canadians including his three eldest sons, and 25 Abenaki warriors. On March 27 they reached the village of Salmon Falls (today Berwick, Maine); 15 men carried out a well-organized attack on a large fortified house, 11 men on a small stockaded fort with bastions, and the rest on the village. The pre-dawn surprise attack was successful; only three attackers were lost, while 34 Anglo-Americans were killed, 54 prisoners taken, and some 29 houses burned down. The alarm had been given, however, and while Hertel's party was withdrawing with its prisoners an Abenaki scout warned that some 100–250 men were pursuing them. In the soon-to-become classic raiders' response to such pursuits, Hertel set up an ambush at the narrow bridge over the Wooster River. When the New England militiamen were crossing the bridge, the Canadians and warriors opened fire from their concealment before charging, yelling war-whoops and wielding tomahawks. Within minutes, 18 pursuers had fallen, including eight killed, and the rest ran off in panic. One Canadian was killed and one of Hertel's sons, Zacharie-François, was wounded.

Hertel's party then went to join up with the third raiding party: 50 Canadians and 60 Abenakis who had left Quebec on January 28 led by René Robineau de Bécancour, Baron de Portneuf, to attack Casco (today Falmouth, Maine). To survive in the winter wilderness they had to hunt game on the way, but in early May they finally reached the Atlantic coast near Casco, and met up with Hertel's party and many additional warriors.

This 19th-century print of Canadian trappers in winter could almost as easily depict raiders of 150 years earlier. They wear *capots* and *mitasses*, and the narrower snowshoes normally used when the snow was not too deep; they drag supplies on a toboggan, and have back-packs supported by the "portage collar" that fitted around the forehead. (After H. P. Share; private collection, author's photo)

The Abenaki nation of Acadia were resolute French allies, whose chief was a French nobleman who had somewhat "gone native," the Baron de Saint-Castin.

Their target was Fort Loyal, a well-built place with four fortified garrison houses and eight cannon guarding the nearby small town. The combined force of Canadians and warriors now probably numbered around 400–500 men. This time, the New England garrison under Capt Davis were aware of their presence before, on May 25, Porneuf's party attacked the town; resistance was stiff, but only Davis and 13 men managed to join the rest of the defenders in Fort Loyal. The next day, Porneuf's men built basic siege works that covered them from artillery fire. On May 29, the attackers pushed a blazing tar barrel close to the fort stockade. The garrison offered to surrender on condition that they could be escorted to an Anglo-American settlement, and Portneuf agreed. Regrettably, his Abenaki allies did not: they burst into the fort to kill or kidnap many prisoners, and only Capt Davis and a handful of other men survived to be taken back to Quebec.

Strategic benefits of raiding tactics

Frontenac, who had learned the principles of strategy and tactics under Marshal Turenne, knew that a "quick and vigorous attack – the strong sword-blow of vengeance – is the most brilliant moment of defense," as later stated by Clauzewitz. It was important for the weaker party to attack his stronger opponent swiftly with, if possible, the element of surprise that was almost sure to bring success and spread dismay. This put the stronger enemy into a defensive posture, and redefined his actual degree of territorial control.

North America at the end of the 17th century was an ideal setting in which to apply these principles. The wild forests separating the French and British colonies were impenetrable to almost anyone except Indigenous warriors – *almost*: and among the exceptions were significant numbers of Canadians, but hardly any Anglo-Americans. (Nobody without experience of such thickly forested terrain can truly appreciate its obstacles, accumulated over centuries and millennia: rocky, uneven ground hidden by deep and slippery leaf-mold and entangling brush, and barred every few yards by rotting deadfall trees.) The 1690 raids had demonstrated that primeval forests become assets of great value to a military force that is able to penetrate them and use them as lines of communication. Such a force could, in effect, make the whole wilderness its own territory, since hardly any of its opponents could travel or fight efficiently in this vast no-man's-land.

The key for a relatively weak New France to become militarily effective had been found, in that raid warfare could keep much more numerous opponents on the defensive. The tactics could be refined, but the basic technique already worked brilliantly. An overwhelming control of the fur trade and great influence over the First Nations were within reach. Frontenac and his successors exploited this relative advantage for as long as raid warfare remained the dominant combat doctrine in North America's wilderness.

Anglo-American attacks on New France, 1690

In the Anglo-American colonies the shock of the early 1690 raids was tremendous, and, as in New France after Lachine, both panic and a hunger for revenge were in the air. New York and the New England colonies came up with a grand plan to invade New France by both land and sea. An army would march from Albany to Montreal via Lake Champlain, while a fleet led by a famous and wealthy sailor, Sir William Phips, would carry troops from Boston to Quebec. This project would be entirely colonial American; no British troops or ships would be involved, and the funding was raised by loans that would be repaid from booty taken in New France. In the early spring Phips had already outfitted eight ships and sailed to Port-Royal, capital of the small French settlements in Acadia (today, Nova Scotia); greatly outnumbered, the town surrendered on May 19.

However, this success did nothing to alleviate the repeated raids on Massachusetts by Saint-Castin and his Abenakis from their safe forest bases, and preparations for the two-prong invasion continued. New York and Connecticut mustered 850 men to march on Montreal under John (or Fitz-John) Winthrop, an Anglo-American veteran of the British Army.

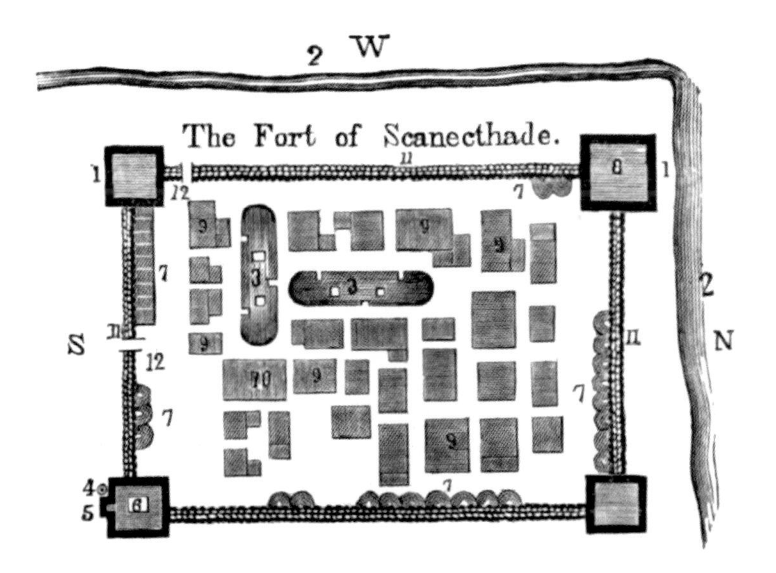

Plan of Schenectady as rebuilt soon after the 1690 raid. Basically unchanged, it was strengthened with triple stockades, and mounted two cannon in each corner blockhouse. The southeast blockhouse has a "spy loft" on top, and a flagpole and sentry-box (4 & 5) outside its southern wall. Among the dwelling-houses are a barn, a blockhouse/church, and, interestingly, two long round-ended "wigwams" (longhouses for First Nations families). In addition to the main gate (12, in the southern wall), there is also a small postern just north of the southwest blockhouse. The constructions numbered 7 along the insides of the stockades are pig-sties. (Print after *A Description of the Province and City of New York... of 1695*, 1862 edn; author's photo)

During the summer they marched north from Albany, but after about 110 miles (180km) the inadequately supplied force halted, weakened by sickness (including smallpox, which frightened Winthrop's Iroquois allies), and turned back with nothing accomplished.

The reputation of New York's troops was somewhat salvaged, however, by a group of militiamen with some knowledge of woodscraft and wilderness fighting, who closely emulated Canadian tactics. Captain Johannes Schuyler led 42 New York volunteers and about 125 Iroquois to the village of Laprairie near Montreal, arriving undetected on August 23. They attacked the surprised inhabitants, killed about six men and much livestock, destroyed 16 houses, then retreated to Albany with 19 prisoners before troops and militiamen could respond.

Much more dangerous to New France was Phips' fleet of at least 34 ships carrying 2,300 militia volunteers from Massachusetts, Rhode Island and New Hampshire towards Quebec. It sailed late due to various delays, and only arrived in view of the capital on October 16. The city presented Phips and his men with an unexpectedly imposing spectacle. On top of the natural fortress of Cape Diamond, Count Frontenac was waiting for them at his château, where he received a New England officer bearing a rather brusque summons to surrender "within an hour." Frontenac told the envoy that his reply would be given "by the mouth of my cannons." Up to

D

WOODLANDS FIRST NATIONS WARRIORS, LATE 17th–MID 18th CENTURY
(1) Summer hunting dress
(2) Winter war dress, 1740s
(3) Ottawa warrior, spring–fall, 1750s

During the second half of the 17th and throughout the 18th century the steady influx of white-men's trade goods, and the displacement and intermixing of some peoples, blurred previous distinctions in Woodlands material culture. Surviving items are often hard to attribute with any certainty, and, unavoidably, this plate shows somewhat "generic" reconstructions from mixed evidence. (The Ottawa warrior **D3** is identified by specifics such as his tattoos, wampum necklaces, and the quillwork decoration of his "bandolier bag.") Clothing was originally of deerskin and the pelts of smaller game animals, but by the end of the 17th century wool and flax (linen) trade cloth was also in common use, as were iron-bladed weapons and "German silver" decorations. Indigenous and imported beads were used for decorating clothing and other items, but in our period imported beads had not yet widely replaced the traditional porcupine-quill and moose-hair work.

The head was sometimes shaved except for a scalp-lock, decorated with feathers, colored animal-hair tufts and/or porcupine quills **(D1 & D3)**. Although trade silver became popular for ear-drops, neck pendants and armbands, the circulation from the Atlantic coast of highly prized white and purple wampum shells for necklaces and other jewelry continued **(D3)**. Tattooing of the face, torso and limbs was common throughout the Algonquian and Iroquoian peoples of the Northeast, supplemented with bold areas of war-paint when appropriate **(D2)**.

The basic dress of First Nations warriors in summer **(D1)** was simply a deerskin or cloth breechclout and hide moccasins, often with hide or cloth *mitasses*; among western and southern groups the latter might be seamed down the front **(D3)** rather than sewn together down the outside leaving flaps or fringes **(D1)**. In cold weather men wore fur robes and caps, or, when active, trade-cloth *capots* **(D2)**. European trade shirts and blankets might be worn in all seasons **(D3)**.

Blankets traded in 17th-century New France were usually white, red or blue, and some were decorated with contrasting stripes "the length of a finger" at the ends, inside a black selvedge **(D3)**. They were generally 5 French feet wide (162cm/63.8in) by 6 feet long (194cm/66.6in). Blankets were important in the fur trade, and were also widely used by Canadian civilians and soldiers alike; they were a vital part of the equipment for any winter raid. In the 18th century the most common colors appear to have been white or red with red or blue stripes, but blue or green blankets were also popular, and there might be many stripes; green blankets made in Toulouse in 1740 had seven or eight stripes **(D2)**.

For hunting and war, the Indigenous peoples had originally used arrows and spears with stone, bone, or antler points, stone blades, and warclubs made from the root-boles of trees **(D2)**. White contact brought first iron knives and hatchets, then tomahawks – which became ubiquitous – guns, powder, and bullet-molds. In the mid-18th century European traders began importing combination tomahawk/tobacco pipes **(D3)**, which answered the needs of both combat and ritual. Trade muskets were usually of relatively smaller caliber than military weapons, and were often decorated with brass furniture. (Michael G. Johnson & Richard Hook, MAA 228 *American Woodland Indians*, Osprey, 1990; Michael G. Johnson & Jonathan Smith, MAA 428 *Indian Tribes of the New England Frontier*, 2006, & MAA 467, *North American Indian Tribes of the Great Lakes*, 2011; Francis Back, "The Trade Blanket in New France" in *The Museum of the Fur Trade Quarterly*, Vol. 26, No. 3, Fall 1990)

1
2
3

The 68-year-old Count Frontenac, dressed as if for Versailles, brandishes a tomahawk in a war-dance with allied First Nations warriors at the great Montreal fur-trade fair in July 1690. (Print after C. W. Jefferys in Doughty's *A Daughter of New France*, 1918; author's photo)

2,800 men, of whom about one-third were regular soldiers, were mustered in defense of the city.

The subsequent artillery duel did not go well for the New Englanders, who finally landed on October 18 in the Beauport area east of the city, where some 1,300 men led by Maj John Walley then lined up with drums beating and colors flying. Some field artillery was also landed, seemingly manned by gunners of Boston's Ancient and Honorable Artillery, which was Walley's own unit. The force marched west, aiming to cross the St Charles River and make a direct assault on the city. However, there was a large wooded area in between. When they approached the woods, marching in ranks, they came under fire from unseen enemies: Frontenac had sent Le Moyne de Sainte-Hélène with 300 Canadians and allied warriors to skirmish against the column. Walley ordered a bayonet charge into the woods, but the skirmishers withdrew from tree to tree, reloading and firing; New Englanders who followed too far became scattered, and fell to tomahawks and knives. Unable to engage effectively, Walley's men finally withdrew.

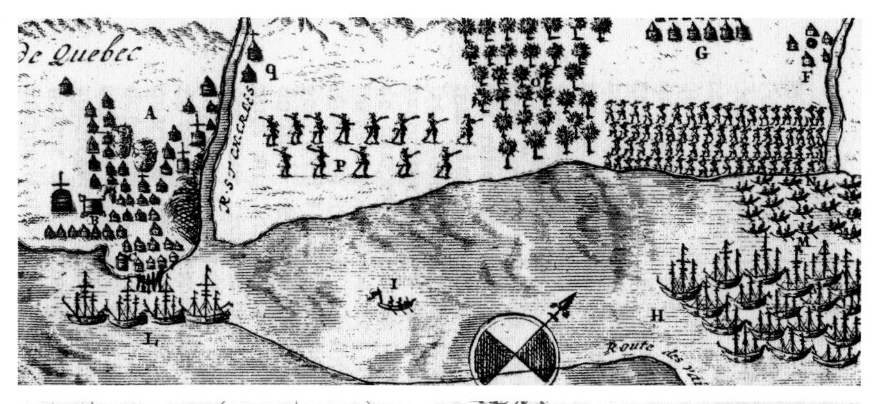

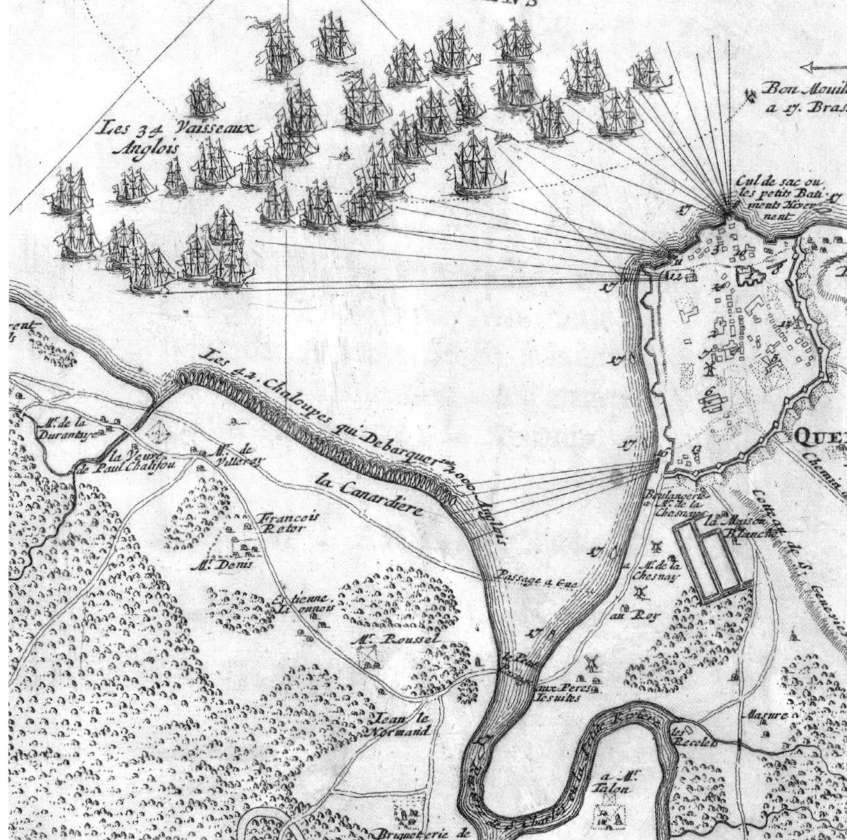

Two schematic maps showing the siege of Quebec in October 1690.

(Upper) Orientated correctly, this shows Quebec City to the west, with the château and Fort St Louis on the headland west of the mouth of the St Charles River, swapping gunfire with Phips' four largest ships. His main fleet is to the east, landing Walley's troops on the Beauport shore, from where they march west towards Quebec. In the left center, Canadian skirmishers and allied warriors go out to meet the New Englanders in the woods. (Detail from a print after La Hontan's 1705 Amsterdam edn; author's photo)

(Lower) A rather more detailed map, but revolved 180° with south at the top; note the longboats beached along the shore at left center, and the arcs of fire from Frontenac's artillery. He had expected an attack from the east, and raised defenses on the riverbank as well as sending his militia forward; Walley's troops never did get across. (Detail from map by Nicolas de Fer; Rijksmuseum, Amsterdam, RP-P-OB-83.033A-122)

During the days that followed they tried again, but never managed to dislodge the skirmishers in spite of hard fighting, during which Sainte-Hélène was mortally wounded. Finally, on the night of October 22, the discipline of the increasingly demoralized and sick New Englanders onshore collapsed when a rumor spread that a huge French attack was imminent; they rushed for their longboats in disorder, and left five brass guns and a color on the beach. Phips and his fleet departed the next day.

The losses are difficult to estimate, but were light for the defenders – perhaps nine dead and eight wounded, plus 44 patients admitted to hospital (for all causes) during the week-long siege. Total Anglo-American losses were much higher: perhaps 600 dead in combat, from sickness, or lost in ships that disappeared during storms on the return voyage. There were great

Not all New England and New York colonists neglected relations with the First Nations. Around the turn of the century the most active among the Mohawks was Pieter Schuyler (1657–1724), first mayor of Albany and colonel of the city's militia, who led a large mixed raid that hit the village of Laprairie de Magdeleine near Montreal in August 1691. The raiders were intercepted during their retreat and took significant losses before they got back to Albany; this was the last sizeable Anglo-American raid into New France for decades to come. In this print after a portrait of *c.*1710 Schuyler wears a red coat and waistcoat, and buff gauntlet gloves. (Private collection; author's photo)

celebrations in Canada, and Louis XIV even had a gold victory coin minted, while near-bankrupt Massachusetts had to print paper money to cover the cost of the failed expedition. Such could be the far-reaching consequences of skillful skirmishing.

Besides brilliantly leading Quebec city's defense, Count Frontenac had already fulfilled his role as a real *Onontio* to the First Nations. He had seen to it that they enjoyed generous terms at the great summer fur-trade fair in Montreal. In July 1690, he was there particularly to greet the Ottawa (Potawatomi) chiefs from the Great Lakes and, at a great assembly, reviewed some 1,200 warriors. He told them that he had long hoped the Iroquois would recognize his affection for them, but that it was not possible to wait any longer. He now hoped all *Onontio*'s allies would "march with us against the Iroquois."

Resisting enemy raids: "the battle of Laprairie," 1691

Small-scale raids continued in 1691, the most remarkable being another strike on Laprairie, led this time by Col Pieter Schuyler of the Albany Militia (elder brother of Capt Johannes Schuyler). The Iroquois were increasingly disappointed by their white allies leaving them to do nearly all the wilderness fighting, so it was important for morale that Schuyler's New York volunteers join them in this summer raid. His force was some 300 strong, half New Yorkers and half Iroquois, mainly Mohawks. Although they were spotted near Chambly, Schuyler's party nevertheless succeeded in surprising a strong detachment of Canadian militiamen camping in a little stockade fort near the St Lawrence River on August 11. In what was remembered as "the battle of Laprairie" Schuyler had two or three killed and about 30 wounded, while French casualties were perhaps double that.

Alerted by the sound of gunfire, regular and militia companies would soon converge on Laprairie. Although it was probably unknown to Col Schuyler, at that time the fur-trade fair was taking place in Montreal, so many allied Ottawa warriors were present besides its garrison. In any event, Schuyler decided to make a rapid retreat to the Richelieu River, where

Speculative reconstruction of a fortified Canadian village, late 17th–early 18th century. As Iroquois raids became more frequent, particularly around Montreal on the southern shore of the St Lawrence, stockades were increasingly built around villages. The main buildings were usually a *seigneur's* house, a church, and a stone-built mill that could also serve as a stronghold. (Print after Edmond J. Massicotte; private collection, author's photo)

his canoes were hidden, but then ran into an ambush set by Capt Philippe de Vallerennes coming up from Fort Chambly with 180 men.

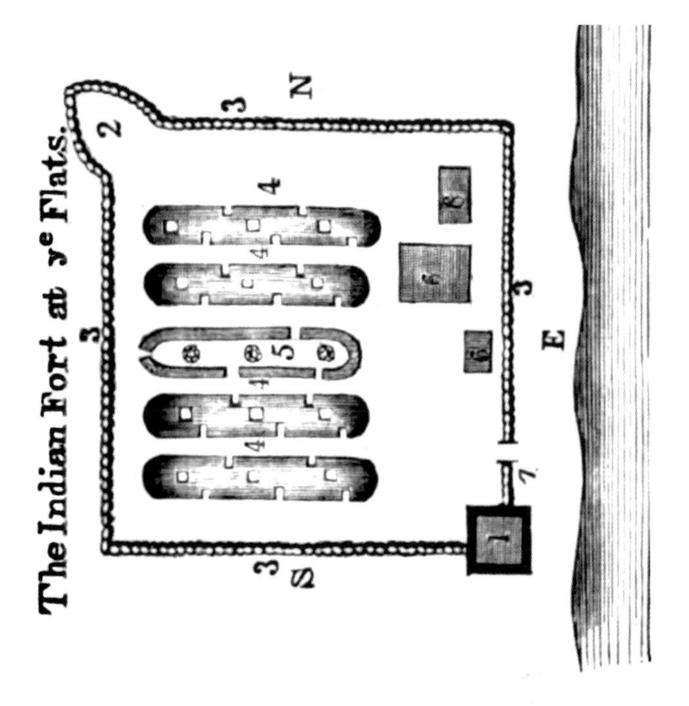

"The Indian Fort at ye Flats." This plan of an Iroquois "castle" in the early 1690s incorporates some European features, such as a blockhouse (but without artillery) in the southeast corner, and houses for use of Anglo-American soldiers inside the eastern stockade. Such a fortified village might hold up to some 60 families, in longhouses; the central one, numbered 5, has had the roof cut away in this drawing to show separate hearths within. (Print after *A Description of the Province and City of New York… of 1695*, 1862 edn; author's photo)

Although Schuyler's force was the stronger, de Vallerennes' men were well positioned behind logs. After a two-hour fight, fearing that other pursuers from Montreal would soon arrive, Schuyler's party "abandoned the battlefield, their baggage and their colors" and made their escape. They were "pursued for three days through swampy country with fallen trees, full of ravines, and none would have escaped if ours [Vallerennes' party] had been stronger," according to La Potherie (II: 141). The French and their allies found the bodies of 83 New Yorkers and 17 Iroquois and suspected that many more were wounded, while reporting only five or six of their own wounded. Back in Albany, Pieter Schuyler and the survivors claimed to have slain over 300 of the enemy including 13 officers (according to Colden, and an obviously incredible figure), for a loss of 43 dead and 25 wounded. Whatever the true numbers, their thinned ranks clearly showed how risky raids deep into Canada had become, due to the speed of the local response. Capt de Vallerennes had pressed Schuyler hard enough to keep him on the run, inflicting casualties and denying him the respite to choose suitable terrain to lay an ambush.

Madeleine de Verchères' fight, 1692

One famous incident during small-scale Iroquois raids into Canada was the fight put up by 14-year-old Madeleine de Verchères, which became iconic in Canadian popular history. She was the daughter of François Jarret de Verchères, a former officer of the Carignan-Salières Regiment who had been granted a *seigneurie* east of Montreal, where he had built a bastioned stockade fort. Sometimes a few soldiers were detached to such "private" forts, but on October 22, 1692 only one soldier was present when an Iroquois war party appeared, and seized about 20 people who were working in the fields.

By her own account, Madeleine was about "400 steps" from the fort. As she ran for it a pursuing Iroquois grabbed at her scarf, but she untied it and slipped free; reaching the fort, she shut its only gate while shouting a call-to-arms. Ignoring several terror-stricken women, she put on the soldier's hat, trying to make it seem as though there were men inside, and then fired a cannon. According to La Potherie, this "struck [the Iroquois] with terror, upset all their calculations and at the same time signaled all the forts on the north and south shores of the river from Saint-Ours as far as Montreal to be on their guard. With each fort passing the word on to the next after the first signal from Verchères … a hundred men were sent to bring it help, who arrived shortly after the Iroquois had disappeared into the woods." The relief detachment caught up with the Iroquois and freed nearly all their prisoners.

When Frontenac's July 1696 expedition against the Onondagas had to disembark at *portages*, the 74-year-old commander "was borne in his canoe by 50 warriors singing and uttering yells of joy." Later on in the march he followed behind the artillery, "borne on a chair, between the two lines" of the central group, "to place himself when he thought proper at the head" of the troops (C11A, 14). His presence ensured high morale, and his tactical eye was unaffected by age. (Courtesy Library and Archives Canada, C6450)

The story was much embellished in Canadian school history books at the end of the 19th century, but the bare facts do show that there was a fairly good organization in place to provide protection. After a cannon-shot set off a chain of alarm signals the raiders could not remain much longer, since relief detachments were numerous and swift in pursuit. Another detail – that Madeleine also fired muskets during the defense, assisted by two younger brothers – confirms that she was familiar with firearms. There are other accounts of Canadian women shooting muskets, for instance at a Maypole during celebrations, as well as when going out hunting, or firing at skulking Iroquois; clearly, Madeleine was far from unique in this ability.

Neutralizing the Iroquois: the Mohawks, 1693

Such raids were not ignored by Governor Frontenac and his officers. After their disastrous failure at Quebec City, the Anglo-American colonists were unlikely to stage another invasion. Frontenac therefore judged this to be an opportune time to neutralize the Iroquois by attacking them in their own territories. They would be challenged and their "castles" destroyed by major expeditions, not only to discourage their raiding but also to degrade their ability to feed themselves.[4]

4 These "castles" were semi-permanent villages of anything between half-a-dozen and 100-plus bark longhouses, surrounded by a palisade up to 30ft high, with fighting platforms and sometimes a ditch, all set amid the clan's corn (maize) fields.

A new factor was that since about the 1660s some Iroquois had been converted to Christianity by French Jesuit missionaries, and were moving to mission villages mostly situated near Montreal. These "Praying Indians of Montreal" were still warriors, however, and would join Canadians in war parties. Again, whatever London had chosen to proclaim, other Iroquois certainly did not think of themselves as British subjects – a warrior was subject to no man – and their attachment to the Anglo-Americans was usually provisional.

Of the five nations then forming the Iroquois confederacy (Mohawks, Oneidas, Onondagas, Cayugas and Senecas), the Mohawks – called *Aigniers* by the French – were the most persistent opponents, because their territory north of Albany was relatively close to Montreal. On January 25, 1693 a 600-strong expedition (100 regular troops, 300 Canadian volunteers and 200 allied warriors) led by lieutenants D'Aillebout de Mantet, Courtemanche, and La Noue left Montreal. Colden writes that "They were well supplied, with all sorts of ammunition, provisions, snowshoes, and such conveniences for carriage as were practicable upon the snow, and through such great forests as they had to pass. The French in Canada have a kind of light sledges made with skins [toboggans], [which] are drawn by large dogs on the frozen snow."

By February 16 the party was spotted in the vicinity of Schenectady and a warning was at once relayed to Albany. The militia was mustered and a troop of cavalry immediately set out to reinforce Schenectady, "but no care was taken to give the Mohawks notice." The raiders surprised two small castles by night, the first when only five men were present with the women

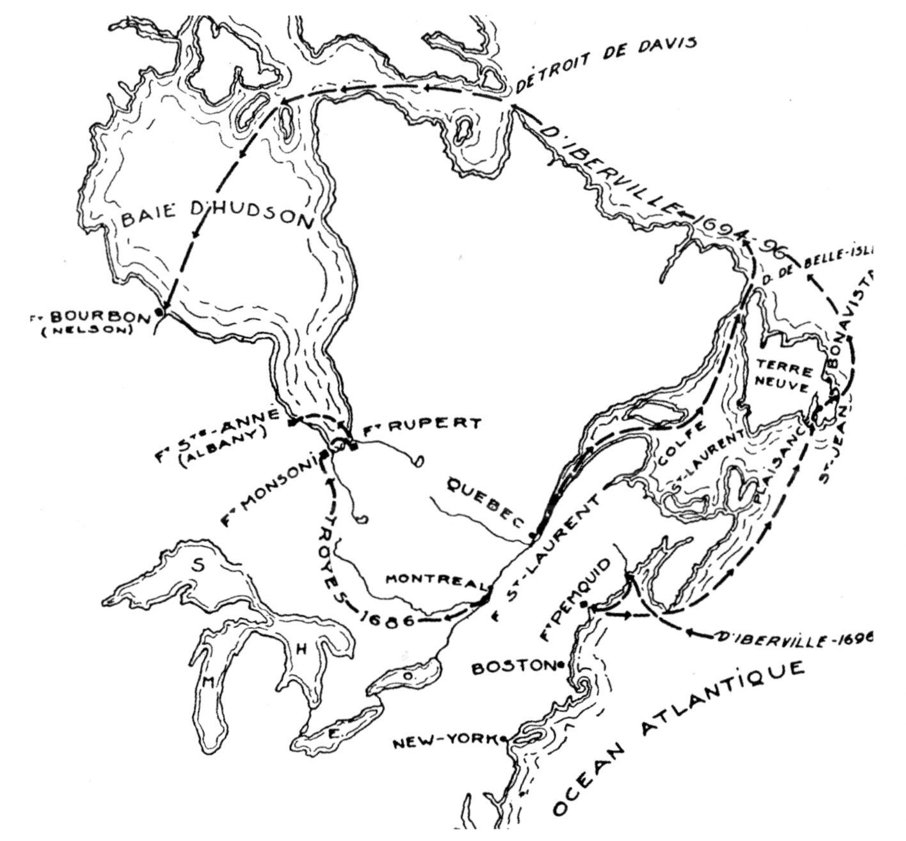

Sketch map showing raids by Pierre de Troyes to James Bay (1686 – "Monsoni" indicates Moose Factory), and raids (1694–96) by Pierre Le Moyne d'Iberville to the coasts of Maine, Newfoundland ("Terre Neuve") and Ft Nelson on Hudson's Bay. D'Iberville with about 50 other Canadians later sailed south to the Caribbean; his last raids were on St Kitt's and Nevis in 1706. (From *Histoire du Canada*, 1912; author's photo)

and children, and both were taken "without any opposition ... being [near to the] English, [they were] not fortified."

The next castle was larger and, as they approached it after dark, the raiders heard war-cries and thought that they had been spotted, but then perceived that a war-dance was being performed by about 40 warriors who were themselves preparing to go raiding. The attackers burst in, and during a savage fight suffered about 30 casualties; while the number of Mohawk warriors killed was unknown, "no doubt it was very considerable," since the party took 300 prisoners including 100 warriors. The longhouses and other structures were all razed and the grain reserves that were found were destroyed. Meanwhile, many Mohawk warriors were at nearby Schenectady when news came of the fall of their castles, and they were "exceedingly enraged" that no New York militiamen went out to assist. At length, Col Pieter Schuyler came out in late March with 200 men, "partly regular troops" later joined by nearly 300 warriors, some "very ill armed," but on hearing that the 600 raiders were withdrawing, he chose prudence.

The Onondaga and Oneida, 1696

Small parties of First Nations allies of the French and British continued to harass their respective enemies with less intensity over the next few years, but in 1696 Frontenac decided to attack the Onondaga nation in strength. Situated inland to the southeast of Lake Ontario, they had raided French traders to seize their furs, and had spurned Frontenac's diplomatic approaches. (Years earlier he had sent a French officer, the Chevalier Pierre d'Aux, on a peace mission to the Onondagas, who had seized him, made him run the gauntlet, and eventually turned him over to the Anglo-Americans,

Impression of D'Iberville leading Canadian militia volunteers in the capture of the forts at St John's, Newfoundland, in November 1696. (Print after Edmond J. Massicotte, 1907; private collection, author's photo)

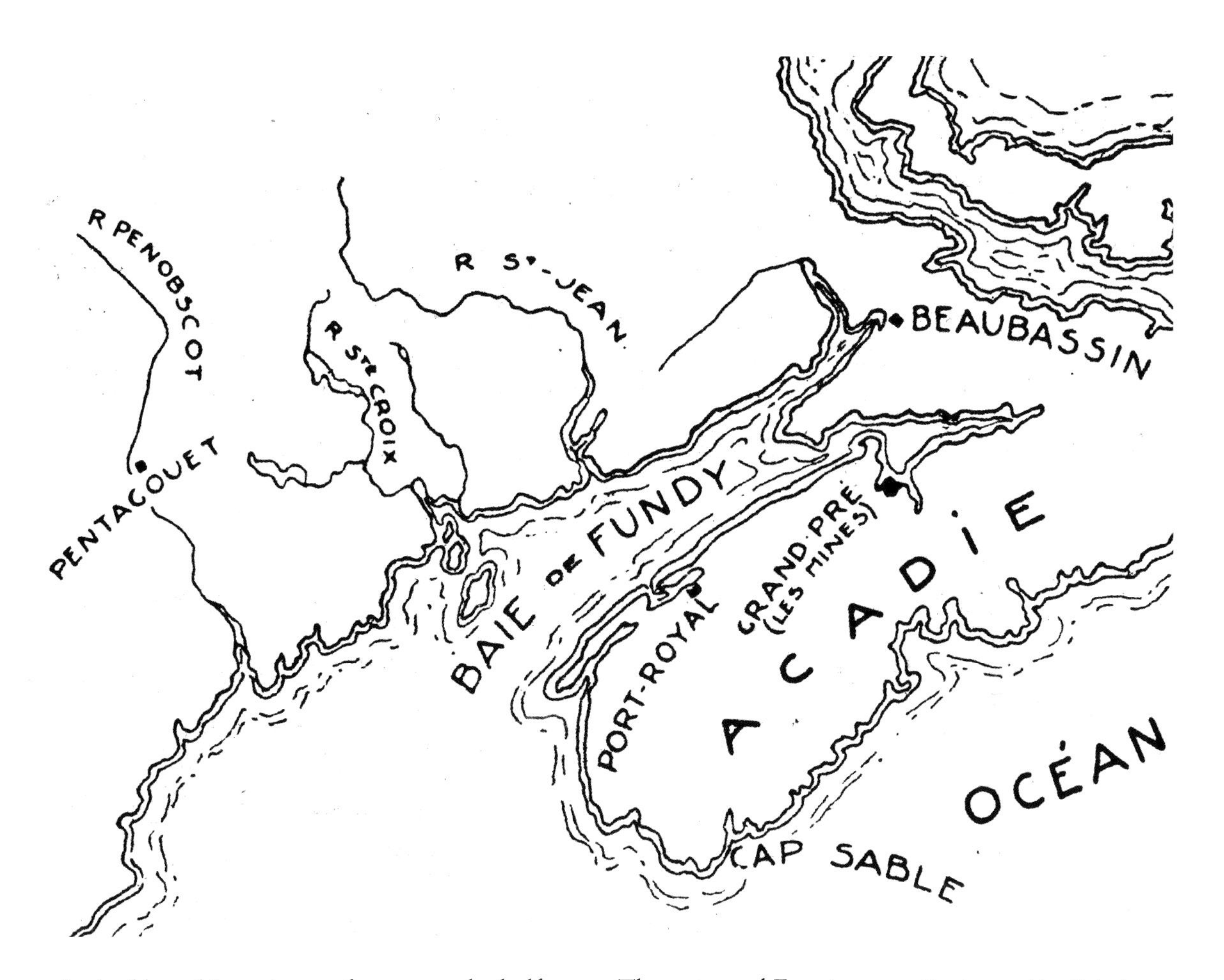

Sketch map of Acadia in the 17th–18th century. The French settlements centered on Port-Royal were established from 1605. Across the Bay of Fundy to the west was "Pentacoet," the base from which Baron de Saint-Castin and the Abenakis launched raids on New England. From 1713 Acadia became the British colony of Nova Scotia, but the borderlands were still held by the French and their allied Indigenous nations; from a main base at Beaubassin many raiding parties still threatened Anglo-American positions in the 1740s and 1750s. (From *Histoire du Canada*, 1912; author's photo)

who had kept him prisoner for two and a half years. The outraged Frontenac had not forgotten this episode.)

In early July 1696 more than 2,200 men left Montreal: about 800 regulars of the *Compagnies franches* and 800-plus Canadian volunteers, all divided into eight battalions, as well as some 500 allied warriors, with two light brass cannon and some light mortars. The force was led by the aged Frontenac in person, although operations were delegated to Callières, Vaudreuil and Ramezay. After a stopover at Fort Frontenac, the force crossed Lake Ontario, landed on July 29, and marched inland. The troops were divided into three groups and not deployed in columns, but rather over a wide front, each battalion being two ranks deep, while allied warriors with some Canadians fanned out as scouts and skirmishers.

Remarkably, no ambushes were encountered during the advance – indeed, no fighting took place at all. Obviously awed by the size of the expeditionary force, the Onondagas evacuated their towns before Frontenac's troops arrived on August 4 and 5. Once he had destroyed both the towns and the crops, he ordered Vaudreuil to take one battalion and some warriors to raze the nearby town and fields of the Oneida nation. There, too, they met no resistance as they destroyed the houses, canoes, standing crops and buried grain reserves – this time, the Onondagas and Oneidas would really starve when winter came. Frontenac withdrew on August 9 and was back in Montreal on the 20th, highly satisfied with all his contingents. When some chiefs at length appeared and complained that their people would have nothing to eat, they were told that *Onontio* was happy to give land to his Iroquois children if they came to live, as others had already, in Canada, where they could feed and lodge themselves safely. Although there had been no fighting, this major summer expedition into Iroquois territory seriously weakened the confederacy. Frontenac, who enjoyed good intelligence, reported to the king on October 25 that the Onondagas and Oneidas "were presently reduced by the lack of food, that would make more perish" than could have been destroyed "by saber and musket." Frontenac had received information that the Mohawks too were suffering from shortages, not only of food but also of arms and ammunition, because "the English" (New Yorkers) had refused to help them (C11A, 14).

Even more important for New France, its friends and foes alike now knew that it could sustain a substantial force in the wilderness in either winter or summer, and therefore could realistically expect victory in almost all raids. The Anglo-American colonies were hemmed in due to their failure to develop appropriate tactics in response, while hostile First Nations, even as far away as the Great Plains, were never quite out of reach of *Onontio*'s soldiers and warriors.

Combined land and sea raids: Pemaquid, 1696

Even before the 1696 expedition, officials both in France and in Canada had considered seaborne attacks on coastal objectives. After the Chevalier d'Aux had finally returned from captivity in 1692, he reported that the New York city area could muster at least 1,100 men besides a company of British regulars, while Boston and its environs had no fewer than 5,000 (C11A, 125). This intelligence deterred landings against such major cities as impractical,

Print of an artist's impression of Governor Louis-Hector de Callières presiding over "the Great Peace of Montreal" with the First Nations in July 1701. The culmination of tireless diplomacy by his predecessor Count Frontenac, this ensured basically peaceful relations for the next 50 years. (From Viator's *Histoire du Canada*, 1915; author's photo)

but small-scale combined operations on weaker and more isolated targets were suggested.

Acadia was the small French colony that had been founded around Port-Royal in today's Nova Scotia in the early 17th century, followed by other minor settlements in present-day New Brunswick and northern Maine, which were repeatedly attacked by privateers from New England. The French settlers had befriended the Abenaki First Nation, while the Massachusetts settlers in Maine regarded them as being close to devil-sent creatures to whom no quarter should be granted. Unsurprisingly, by about 1675 the Abenaki warriors had become the most redoubtable defenders of the Acadian borderlands. Twenty years later they were led by the extraordinary Jean-Vincent d'Abadie, Baron de Saint-Castin (1652–1707). This French nobleman and ex-officer had been adopted by the Abenakis, marrying one of their "princesses" and becoming a chief. Combining both European and Indigenous concepts of warfare, he had turned the Abenakis into the most formidable force northeast of Massachusetts. He had Fort Pentagoet as a base for trade, arms, and supplies, and a few other white adventurers and missionaries often accompanied him on Abenaki raids.

The most important of several forts built by the Massachusetts settlers was Fort Charles at Pemaquid (today Pemaquid Beach, Maine). It was normally garrisoned by about 50 trained militiamen, but in August 1689 barely 16 men were present when hundreds of Abenakis took the fort and the adjoining village.[5] Lt James Weems described the attackers as "all well-armed with French fuzees, waist belts and cutlasses, and most of them with bayonets and pistols, gray and black hats on their heads, and some of them with colored wigs" (compare with Plate E).

This defeat left some 200 miles (300km) of the coast defenseless. The colony's answer was to rebuild a new, much stronger masonry fort at Pemaquid for the sum of £20,000 – one-third of Massachusetts' annual budget – during 1692. Called Fort William Henry, this had a permanent garrison of about 90 men and 20 cannon, and was (foolishly) proclaimed to be impregnable. In 1696, it offered a tempting target for a combined sea and land operation to the Canadian officer Pierre Le Moyne d'Iberville, by now a French Navy captain.

Saint-Castin mobilized his warriors, while D'Iberville arrived in Acadian waters with three warships; he anchored off Fort Pentagoet on August 7, to be greeted by Saint-Castin with about 250 Abenakis. The warriors went overland to invest Fort William Henry, soon being joined offshore by D'Iberville's ships. On August 15 the fort's commander, one Capt Pasco Chubb (who was known to have treacherously murdered Indigenous people in cold blood) pompously replied to a surrender summons by declaring that he would never capitulate even "if the sea was covered with French ships and the woods full of French and savages."

D'Iberville promptly landed some cannon and mortars for two siege batteries, and ordered a few mortar shells to be fired into the fort. These were followed by a second summons, stating that if the defenders capitulated at once they would be safely evacuated, but if they persisted until the fort was breached there could be no quarter, since it would be impossible to

5 For details of the American colonial militias, see Men-at-Arms 366, 372 & 383, *Colonial American Troops 1610–1774 (1), (2) & (3)*. New England and New York are covered in MAA 372.

restrain the Abenakis. Pressed by his terrified garrison, Chubb surrendered. The prisoners were escorted to safety by French marines, and the fort was destroyed. (The warriors were disappointed at not killing Chubb, especially after they had found in the fort a starving Abenaki chained in a cell, but they finally caught up with him two years later during a raid on Andover, Massachusetts.) After delivering the Pemaquid prisoners to Boston, D'Iberville's squadron sailed away, and worried colonists as far away as New York wondered where it would strike next.

Newfoundland, 1696–97

D'Iberville reappeared off Newfoundland and anchored at Placentia, the capital of its French southern coast. Newfoundland had great economic importance due to its then extraordinary fishing industry; its coasts were studded with mainly French and British anchorages for ships that went out to the nearby Grand Banks. In Placentia, D'Iberville joined its governor, Jacques-François de Montebon de Brouillan, in a plan to destroy the British Newfoundland settlements and fisheries. D'Iberville wanted expert winter raiders, and at his request Frontenac sent him 124 picked Canadian volunteers from Quebec. On October 29, 1696 Governor Brouillan set out by sea with part of the *Compagnie franche* based at Placentia, while D'Iberville's party departed overland on November 1 for the British capital, St John's.

They joined forces at Ferryland, some 50 miles (80km) south of St John's, whose outskirts they reached on November 28. The Canadian advance guard immediately attacked during a snowstorm, overwhelming about 80 defenders in advanced posts. Led by D'Iberville in person, they then assaulted and took two small forts, and were about to attack the main fort when it surrendered on November 30. The forts and part of the town were destroyed, and over the next four months the Canadians under Jacques Testard de Montigny benefited from their snowshoes and winter clothing to mount constant raids on the English fisheries. Only Bonavista and Carbonear still flew the Union flag when the attackers withdrew in March 1697, leaving the British Newfoundland fisheries ruined.

London immediately dispatched Gibson's Regiment of Foot (subsequently, the 28th) with gunners and engineers to rebuild and secure St John's. However, it would fall to France again late in 1704, recaptured by a force that included detachments of Canadians, warriors, and some 300 French Basque fishermen. (It is recorded that these were equipped

E

AMBUSH OF ALBANY DRAGOONS, 1707

During both "King William's War" (1689–97) and "Queen Anne's War" (1702–13), small parties of warriors from the so-called Wabanaki Confederacy of the Abenaki, Passamaquoddy and Micmac peoples routinely preyed on the outskirts of Anglo-American communities, and there are several accounts of their ambushing militia troopers who rode to the rescue. Here we attempt to reconstruct one remarkable clash that occurred in 1707 and was reported in the *Mercure Galant* that November. When a few Abenaki warriors were detected on the outskirts of Albany, the alarm was sounded. Blue-coated Albany Dragoons **(E1)** got to horse and galloped in pursuit of the running warriors, who retreated into woodland. As the riders came up, other hidden warriors opened fire on them from the edge of the trees in what was obviously a deliberately planned ambush. During the five-hour running fight that followed, the Albany militiamen never succeeded in catching up with the elusive warriors, who eventually vanished – taking some scalps with them, and seemingly suffering no casualties themselves.

Even before the turn of the 17th/18th centuries the French are recorded as giving some warriors, including Abenakis, hats and old uniform coats, and **(E2)** wears that of a 1690s drummer of the *Compagnies franches*. In the 1680s–90s the Abenaki also received some French military accoutrements, such as belts with swords and plug bayonets **(E4)**. Hoods extending over the shoulders were characteristic of the dress of the Abenaki and associated nations **(E3)**, originally made of birch bark or leather, and later of trade cloth.

3
2
1
4

in the Canadian style with *tapabord* caps, powder horns, bullet pouches worn across the shoulder, snowshoes, and toboggans.) Newfoundland only became entirely British, alongside Nova Scotia, in 1713 following the Treaty of Utrecht.

The "Great Peace of Montreal," 1701

Small incursions continued in the New France and New England borderlands, but with less intensity, especially after it was learned that the war between France and Britain had ended in Europe. Just as importantly, the seeds of Frontenac's diplomacy were bearing fruit and, after his death at Quebec on November 28, 1698, Louis-Hector de Callières ably assumed the mantle of governor-general. He presided in the summer of 1701 over a gathering at Montreal of some 1,300 chiefs and warriors from more than 30 First Nations, including the Iroquois, which concluded a general peace treaty. This "Great Peace of Montreal" was a diplomatic coup for New France, and it essentially held until the outbreak of the Seven Years' War 50 years later. With the Iroquois more or less neutralized, and the Anglo-Americans neither eager nor usually very effective raiders, the Canadians and their Indigenous allies were left as more or less the masters of the wilderness.

"Queen Anne's War," 1702–13

The War of the Spanish Succession, called "Queen Anne's War" by Anglo-Americans, broke out in 1702, and inevitably found France and Britain once again on opposite sides. In Quebec city, staff officers pondered as to what raids would be most effective, while the Anglo-American colonies called in vain for Britain to conquer New France with conventional armies and fleets. In 1703 Philippe de Rigaud, Marquis de Vaudreuil (1650–1725) became governor-general of New France. Trained in the King's Musketeers before going on to hold commands in several European campaigns, he had arrived in Canada in 1687 as commander of its *Compagnies franches de la Marine*. Vaudreuil approved of the tactical plans promoted by many of his officers, but this time there would be no expeditions against the Iroquois; all raids would be on the English colonies. These began modestly into Maine in August 1703, and also in the Connecticut River valley.

Deerfield, 1704

For Canadians this would be just another large winter raid, but in New England it became one of the most notorious in colonial history.

On the evening of March 10, 1704, a party of 200 Abenaki and Iroquois mission warriors with 50 Canadians under the command of Lt Jean-Baptiste Hertel de Rouville were spying, undetected, on the village of Deerfield, which had a garrison of 20 Massachusetts soldiers. Thinking everything "then still and quiet," no watch was posted, and all went to bed. Two hours before daylight, the raiders attacked "the Fort and by the advantage of some drifts of snow, got over the walls" and broke down doors. In the confused fighting that followed some 48 Anglo-Americans were killed and about 100 taken prisoner; three raiders were killed, and Lt Hertel was among 20 others who were wounded. After plundering and burning the village, Hertel withdrew on March 12. By then the alarm had spread and militiamen tried to pursue, but when the raiders counterattacked and slew nine of them the others fled. The next day many more militiamen were in the area but, according to Penhallow, they did not venture into the woods due to their lack of snowshoes. The raiders made it back safely to Montreal with more than 100 captives.

Haverhill, 1708

This summer raid, on a village just 30 miles (50km) north of Boston, provides an example both of the remarkably long distances that some expeditions were prepared to cover, and of defensive measures among small Anglo-American communities.

The raiding party led by Capt Jean-Baptiste de Saint-Ours Deschaillons and (again) Lt Hertel de Rouville consisted of about 100 soldiers and Canadians, with a "dozen young officers" who had joined it as volunteers to acquire first-hand experience, plus more than 200 allied warriors. The original target was Portsmouth, New Hampshire, but this was abandoned due to sickness breaking out amongst the allied warriors, of whom all but about 50 departed. With the force reduced by half, attacking Portsmouth was now out of the question, and a smaller community was chosen instead.

Jean-Baptiste Hertel de Rouville (1668–1722), *c.*1710. Despite the impression given by the stiff conventions of 18th-century portraiture (including an odd rendering of a steel breastplate, although armor had been abandoned by fighting men in New France since the 1640s), this son of François Hertel de la Fresnière was an experienced bush fighter from his teenage years, and notably led the raids on Deerfield (1704) and Haverhill (1708). De Rouville was made a knight of the Order of Saint-Louis in December 1721, and its cross was later painted onto the portrait. (Print after portrait; private collection, author's photo)

According to Deschaillons' report, the party "surmounted a thousand difficulties, and had traveled nearly 480 miles (770km) by paths so difficult that it surpasses imagination" before they finally got to Haverhill. This was a "village consisting of about 25 to 30 houses, with a timber fort" garrisoned by some 30 Boston provincial militiamen, besides others billeted in various houses. On August 29, 1708, the raiders attacked half an hour before dawn, taking the fort by surprise and setting fire to it and all the houses. It was difficult to estimate the defenders' losses, "because the English who were shut in them would not come out and fired continuously on our party."

Since there were four other forts and villages in the vicinity, and the raiders could hear in the distance the sound of "trumpets and drums" mustering militiamen, they soon withdrew. Before long the area was "filled with horsemen and men on foot," who followed the raiders for some distance. The raiders retired in good order, but after about 1.5 miles (2.5km), as they approached a wood, they were ambushed by 60 to 70 Massachusetts men who fired a volley at them. This was clearly not very effective, as the raiders dumped their packs and charged, jumping over "a sort of fence that provided their cover" and striking "at anything that looked English ... [in] so rough a manner" that they ran off. The Canadians and warriors only stopped pursuing the fleeing militiamen when "they reached the first houses," after which all the raiders resumed their retreat, abandoning part of their baggage. They reported ten men killed including three warriors and two young officers, and 18 wounded (C11A, 28). The Massachusetts casualties were about 30 to 40 killed and wounded. Nevertheless, this lesson in the risks of making very deep raids, on a population that was generally on its guard (despite its local carelessness over posting sentries), was not forgotten in New France.

These famous raids were just two of at least 30 substantial expeditions during the war which involved regular officers, Canadians and warriors, besides attacks by small Indigenous parties on villages even in the suburbs of Albany or Boston. Pursuing Anglo-American militiamen were almost totally ineffective, and, according to the January 1705 *Mercure Galant*, Canadians joked that their "bellies full of beer" prevented them from walking fast enough. Even if pursuing cavalrymen did catch up, it might well be their last ride (see Plate E).

A war club of the Fox and Sauk nations, mounting a steel blade. Termed a "gunstock club" from its shape, this type of weapon was carried by warriors of many Indigenous nations from the later 17th century, and this example was recorded by the traveler and artist Karl Bodner as late as the 1830s. (Print after Bodner; private collection, author's photo)

On the whole, Canada had become nearly invulnerable to Anglo-American land raids or troop movements, but the colonists still had hopes of striking effectively by sea. However, when they were shipped to attack Port-Royal in Acadia in 1707, some 1,300 Massachusetts provincial troops were repulsed by about 150 defenders in a series of fiascos. In 1710, this time with the help of the Royal Navy, about 2,000 British and provincial troops finally overcame Port-Royal's resistance, and it surrendered on October 1. With this encouragement, in summer 1711 forces gathered north of Albany, while Adm Hoveden Walker led a fleet with 7,500 British and provincial troops on board to attack Quebec city. It might have worked; but on August 22, in bad visibility, strong winds and currents drove the fleet against the northern shore of the Gulf of St Lawrence near the Isle aux Oeufs, sinking eight ships and drowning some 900 soldiers and sailors. The fleet withdrew, and the overland attempt was also abandoned.

The Fox Wars, 1712–37

In the late 17th century the Fox nation (also called Renard, Outagamis and Mesquakies) lived in present-day Wisconsin. They were a warrior people who detested the French, and were traditional enemies of nearly all the First Nations allied to New France. From 1701, when the French established their large post at Detroit, tensions rose. An attempt by the Fox to take Detroit in May 1712 was defeated, but they continued to prey upon New France's vital fur-trade routes. Once again, raiding expeditions against them employed the well-proven combination of French troops, Canadians and allied warriors, but the challenges were even greater than for the former operations against the Iroquois. There were relatively few French soldiers of the *Compagnies*

ASSAULT EQUIPMENT, 1730s
(1) Plan for mantlet construction
(2) Mantlet in action
(3) Wheeled extendable ladder

During the Fox Wars in the first third of the 18th century, more elaborate devices than battering-rams were used. The Fox or Mesquakie ("red earth people") – originally from around the Fox and Wolf rivers and Lake Winnebago, and later reported around Green Bay, Wisconsin – built some remarkable defenses to resist the French raiders and their allies, perhaps being inspired by European examples. Against Indigenous communities surprise attacks were next to impossible, so, intriguingly, the French resorted to quasi-medieval technology to cope with these challenging fortifications. As early as 1613 the explorer Champlain had used wooden towers to enable his matchlock musketeers to shoot down inside Iroquois "castles," and the same approach was adopted against the Fox in 1712 and 1730. The engineer Chaussegros de Léry, who took part in the Fox Wars, recommended in a memoir of 1739 the use during attacks of wheeled mantlets with protective planking **(frame as F1)** to shelter men approaching a rampart or gateway under fire **(F2)**, and extendable ladders mounted on wheeled turrets **(F3)** to get assault parties inside. Since these "siege engines" had to be constructed on the spot with axe and saw, their actual appearance was probably less precisely finished than in the engineer's drawings. Typical campaign dress for the *Compagnies franches* is illustrated, though we choose to show the sergeant in F2 wearing the regulation *justaucorps* coat and carrying his sword, and the leading attacker in F3 is a Canadian "woods-runner." (LAC, microfilm 559)

1
2
3

There are occasional references to the pre-1789 plain white standard of France (without the gold lilies sometimes shown by later artists) being supplied for raiding parties – for instance, "a standard of Lyon linen with its pole" carried by each of three parties "going to war" against the Fox in 1728 (AC, F1A, 27) – and some were also given to First Nations. A white fighting flag was flown by French warships, and when enemy vessels sought to surrender they too raised a white flag; this practice became so widespread that a white flag signifies surrender to this day. (Print after late 17th-century MS; private collection, author's photo)

franches in the western forts, and Canadian *coureurs-des-bois* were also less numerous on this far-flung frontier. The distances were enormous, and the Fox villages were strongly fortified. In 1716 an 800-strong mixed force imposed a peace that lasted for some years, but by 1728 war had resumed after Canadian traders had again been killed. Strong expeditions were sent out, Fox villages were stormed and destroyed (see Plate F), and some 900 had been killed by the end of 1730. Still not totally defeated, the Fox were helped by the neighboring Sauk nation. Despite losing hundreds more killed or enslaved by French-allied warriors, they continued to resist. Both the remaining Fox and the Sauk were pursued as far as present-day Iowa in 1735, but were not caught. Governor Beauharnois "pardoned" both nations in 1737, and sent a French officer to live among them in Iowa the following year.

THE FINAL CAMPAIGNS, 1740s–50s

"King George's War," 1744–48: Raids on New England, 1745–46

The outbreak of the War of the Austrian Succession in Europe in 1743, which as always pitted France against Britain, brought a resumption of raiding from New France against the British colonies during "King George's War."

The spectacular fall of the French fortress of Louisburg on Isle Royale (Cape Breton Island) in 1745 had no major effect on Canada's defenses, but it encouraged keeping up pressure on the enemy's colonies. A summary of the various raiding parties that left Montreal between December 1745 and August 1746 gives an idea of the tempo of operations. Eight large expeditions, half of them between December and March, were sent to raid the New

England and New York borders. Led by regular officers, with Canadian volunteers and up to 1,000 First Nations warriors, these are occasionally mentioned in American histories (for instance, the 600-strong raid that burned Saratoga on November 28, 1745).

Analysis of the documents further reveals that about 30 to 35 smaller raiding parties of Abenakis and allied "Praying Iroquois" warriors were provided with supplies, for instance a party of 20 Abenaki that "set out towards Boston, and brought in some prisoners and scalps" (C11A, 85). Together these parties totaled at least 1,000 warriors, who raided with such success that the colonists were obliged to keep large numbers of militiamen mustered for defense. Thus at least 2,000 French-allied warriors were involved in the whole spectrum of raids during a period of eight months.

Annapolis-Royal, 1744 & 1746–47

Following the 1713 Treaty of Utrecht, Acadia had become the British colony of Nova Scotia, though still for the time being populated with French settlers. Port-Royal had been renamed Annapolis-Royal, and its fort had become Fort Anne, garrisoned by 150 men of the British 40th Foot. In September 1744 an attempt on Fort Anne was made by a small French seaborne expedition from Fortress Louisburg, but this withdrew after a three-week blockade.

After the fall of Louisburg the following year, in 1746 a party from Canada led by *Commandant* Ramezay arrived in the area. Finding Annapolis-Royal too strong, after a short blockade the force withdrew to over-winter at the wilderness raiders' base of Beaubassin. In December reinforcements arrived at Annapolis-Royal from Boston, consisting of 450 New England provincial troops under the command of LtCol Arthur Noble, of whom about half were billeted in civilian homes at nearby Grand-Pré.

Ramezay sent 600 men under Capt Antoine Coulon de Villiers to raid Grand-Pré; half were Canadians, and the others Acadians who had abandoned their homes, and warriors who remained loyal to the French. On February 10, 1747, after a difficult 11-day trek on snowshoes, the undetected raiders were within sight of their target. That night a strong blizzard blew up, and (yet again) the New Englanders posted no sentries. Divided into ten assault groups of about 50 men each, the raiders surrounded ten houses

FAR LEFT
Once again, readers should not be deceived by the powdered hair and fictional armor in the conventional officer portraits on these pages: these were all fighting men with experience in the wilderness. Philippe Testard de Montigny (1724–86), born in Montreal, entered the *Compagnies franches* in 1736 as a 12-year-old cadet at the frontier fort of Michilimackinac, and was later commissioned. A veteran of numerous engagements including Monongahela (1755) and Oswego (1756), he was captured at Niagara in 1759. Like many Canadian officers, he chose to retire to France rather than remain in his native country after it was ceded to Britain. (Print after original portrait; private collection, author's photo)

LEFT
Charles Deschamps de Boishébert (1727–97). The son of an officer, in 1739 (so again only 12 years old) he was already an officer-cadet, and was commissioned in the *Compagnies franches* in 1741–42. Although he was at Detroit in 1748 and on the Ohio in 1753, he served mainly on the border of Nova Scotia, participating in many raids under Ramezay during the later 1740s including that on Grand-Pré. Later, leading a mixed wilderness force of soldiers, Canadians and warriors, he kept the British on permanent alert as far as Halifax. The ruthless British deportation of the French Acadian population in 1755 brought to his camp many volunteers eager for revenge. Boishébert went back to Canada in late 1758; knighted, in 1759 he led a party of Acadian volunteers against the British at Quebec. After the capitulation of French forces in September 1760 he too emigrated to France, where his looks earned him the nickname *"le beau canadien."* (Print after an original portrait, c.1765; private collection, author's photo)

RIGHT
Charles Le Moyne, second Baron de Longueuil (1687–1755). Scion of the influential Le Moyne family, he was educated in Rochefort, France, as a naval midshipman, and was commissioned into the Canadian *Compagnies franches* in 1713. Revealing a talent for command and administration, he was made commandant of the important Fort Niagara in 1726, became town major of Montreal in 1733, and was knighted in the Order of Saint-Louis in 1734. In 1739–40 he led 442 men, including 319 allied warriors, on an expedition to Louisiana which pacified the hostile Chickasaw nation through the use of Canadian tactics. He was named acting governor-general of New France in 1752; here the artist's rendering of his body-armor is particularly unconvincing. (Print after an original portrait, c.1750; private collection, author's photo)

FAR RIGHT
Luc La Corne de Saint-Luc (1711–84) was both an officer of the *Compagnies franches* and a successful fur trader who spoke four or five aboriginal languages. He spent part of his life in the wilderness as an outstanding leader of First Nations warriors, making many successful raids during the 1740s and 1750s. After the capitulation he reconciled himself to British rule, and was considered a man of "first property and consequence" by the British governor Sir Guy Carleton. He even led Indigenous warriors in Gen Burgoyne's disastrous 1777 campaign during the American Revolutionary War; held blameless for the defeat, he was appointed ADC by Governor Haldiman. La Corne was not alone amongst the Canadian gentry in his choice; another veteran of frontier outposts and expeditions in the 1740–50s, Charles-François Tarieu de Lanaudière, chose to return from France to Canada in 1763, and was also named an ADC by Carleton. (Print after original portrait, c.1765; private collection, author's photo)

where 220 of Noble's men were sleeping, and attacked in the pre-dawn darkness. Colonel Noble and about 140 of his men were killed and another 34 wounded; the rest, isolated in a stone house, surrendered the next day. The raiders suffered only six killed and 14 wounded. In a touch of 18th-century gallantry, Villiers and his officers hosted a dinner for the captured officers, and the garrison were granted the honors of war.

The "French-Indian War," 1754–60

The North American campaigns of the global Seven Years' War (1754–63) were sparked by the "Jummonville Incident," and the retaliatory capture of Fort Necessity from George Washington's Virginia provincial troops by a force of French, Canadians and First Nations allies. By now, New France's population had grown to some 55,000, but that of the Anglo-American colonies to about 1.5 million. Substantial regular reinforcements were shipped out from both France and Britain, and both waged the war largely in as "conventional" a manner as the local conditions allowed. Perhaps the summit of Canadian raid-warfare tactics was achieved at the battle of Monongahela on July 9, 1755, when Gen Braddock's British column was destroyed by forest ambushers.[6]

Braddock's successor, the Earl of Loudon, was a talented commander who recognized that the British forces had to be able to field the equivalent of New France's raiders. He created both American colonial "Ranger" units, and the British Army's first regular light infantry regiment, Gage's 80th Regiment "of Light Armed Foot." Initially neither was the equal of their experienced opponents, but Loudon's initiative certainly signaled that, at last, the British and Anglo-Americans were squarely addressing the challenge.

Conversely, officers of the French metropolitan troops sent to Canada from 1755 largely spurned the Canadians' "*sauvage*" way of war, preferring European linear tactics. Consequently, the deciding factor was that Britain was willing to commit overwhelming force in North America, but France was not. All French forces capitulated in September 1760, and Canada was ceded to Britain in 1763, bringing the era of New France's raiders to an end.

6 See Men-at-Arms 48, *Wolfe's Army*; and Campaign 140, *Monongahela 1754–1755*

A Canadian volunteer lighting his pipe during a winter trek. This 19th-century engraving could easily depict a wilderness fighter from New France during the two preceding centuries. He wears a *capot* with its hood up over his wool cap, a waist sash, winter moccasins, and the wide snowshoes suitable for deep snow, and his weapon is covered to protect it. Only the moustache is unlikely: since Indigenous people disliked facial hair, which was also out of fashion in Europe by the end of the 17th century, Canadians of our period were almost always clean shaven. (Print after A. Dupuy; private collection, author's photo)

MEN, EQUIPMENT & METHODS

Officers and men

Officers provided the diplomatic link with the First Nations that attracted them to the French cause. The early promoters of the new tactical doctrine, such as Le Moyne and Hertel, had become familiar with Indigenous languages and lifestyles either as traders or prisoners. Once the *Compagnies franches de la Marine* became the permanent garrison of New France, the young French officer-cadets' training included a residence with an allied nation to learn its language and culture, and many volunteered for raiding expeditions. Within a couple of decades the officer-cadets were usually the Canadian-born sons of the original officers, who then came to form the great majority of the regular officer corps in New France before 1755. They had a French education and training, and this dual legacy enabled them to provide the professional but locally experienced leadership required in raid warfare.

While the enlisted men of the Independent Naval Companies were recruited in France, many of them became attracted to life in the Canadian settlements, which offered many freedoms denied to Frenchmen at home under the *Ancien Régime*. Billeted in inhabitants' homes, they often found love in the arms of Canadian girls and became settlers themselves. Others discovered a taste for postings in far-away forts. All soldiers in those stations were allowed some private trading with the First Nations, and this provided the means to accumulate some savings for when they came back to Montreal after the usual three-year tour. Some soldiers in these distant postings became so accustomed to frontier life that they never did come back. The gunner "J.C.B." met some at Michilimackinac, including one who had been there for 30 years. The soldiers on the frontier often adopted features of the Indigenous lifestyle and became experts in forest-craft. Such men were ideal for the picked parties of regulars who could withstand, like Canadian *coureurs-des-bois* and *voyageurs*, the hardships of raid warfare.

Material culture: Canadian dress

To fully understand the military success of the New France raiders, one also has to consider the arms, equipment, and especially the clothing that they used. The latter was a practical adaptation that enabled them to fight, at any time of the year, after traveling significant distances through a trackless wilderness, in near-Arctic winter conditions or through dense primeval forest in summer.

The regular Naval troops posted in Quebec, Trois-Rivières and Montreal, as well as forts in the Richelieu River valley and major garrisons such as Forts Frontenac and Niagara, or large settlements such as Detroit, wore European-style uniform (see Plate C1). But such uniforms proved useless for long wilderness expeditions, so, to quote Philippe Aubert de Gaspé, officers and men alike took to wearing the "short *capot*, *mitasses*, breechclouts and deerskin shoes [moccasins]. This practical and light equipment gave them a great advantage over enemies dressed in the European fashion" (see Plates A1, C2 & C3). Such adaptation by French settlers to the Canadian environment started in the first half of the 17th century, in a distinct costume that was a mixture of French maritime and First Nations features. Typical dress and equipment did not change markedly from the middle of the 17th until well into the 18th century, though details such as cuffs and pockets might be influenced by French fashion.

Canadians (see Plate B) usually wore a wool cap of "stocking" shape, generally either red, white or blue; better-quality caps might be trimmed with fur, especially for colder weather. Another type was the *tapabord*, a round

G

RIVER TRANSPORT, *c.*1700

The vast network of rivers served as the roads of New France, and from spring to late fall canoes were the essential means for transporting men, arms, supplies and goods by soldiers, Canadians and First Nations alike. While the essential techniques and materials used for making the light, strong birchbark canoes were common to all, the profiles of bow and stern favored by particular Indigenous peoples and the Europeans who worked with them might differ. So too did the size; the largest carried about a metric ton's weight of cargo, and accommodated up to 14 paddlers. The example we illustrate seems to have been the main type employed for trade and expeditions, and follows, for instance, the dimensions of three that were ordered by the government in June 1700. These were to be 30ft long (9.7m) by 4ft 1in wide (1.3m), the bottom being reinforced with pine planks, and with eight thwarts or cross-planks for paddlers to sit on. They would paddle for anything from eight to 14 hours a day, using their folded *capots* as seat cushions; the man in the bow acted as the pilot, and the man in the stern used his paddle as a rudder. (Here, the bow man has tattoos and a quill-decorated sash, suggesting long experience among the First Nations.) A sail might also be rolled around a dismounted mast and lashed along one side, to take advantage of favorable winds.

"Habillemens des Coureurs de bois Canadiens." This unsigned drawing of *c.*1730 is a unique period view of Canadian wilderness clothing in late spring or summer. All wear short *capots* fastened by waist sashes. One (left) has breeches, *mitasses*, and apparently boot-moccasins, while the others have very wide skirt-like breechclouts and are bare-legged and barefoot, as was more likely when in often damp canoes. Pipe-smoking was very common. Bullet bags and (right) a tomahawk are carried from the sashes, and one (center) has a slung powder horn. The muskets appear to be (from left to right) a long "buccaneer" type, a shorter "half-buccaneer," and a hunting or trade model. (Courtesy Beinecke Library, Yale University, New Haven, CT; object 2001154)

cap featuring a visor (peak) that could be turned up in front, and side and rear flaps that could be tied up above the crown or let down (see Plate A). Linen shirts were worn by all, or woolen shirts in winter. A neckcloth of linen or satin material might be worn by soldiers and militiamen.

The *capot* was a warm and ample woolen coat originally used by French sailors. In Canada its cut was more fitted, resembling the European *justeaucorps* coat, but without pocket flaps or many buttons. It came in several versions and lengths, the most common with knee-length skirts. A shorter style, presumably favored in warmer weather, reached only to the mid-thigh, while longer winter versions might reach low on the calves. *Capots* usually fastened across the breast to a button on the upper right side, though some might button down the front; buttons were of metal, leather, or cloth-covered wood or bone. Turnback "boot" cuffs, buttoned at the top as on European coats, seem to have been common, but cuffs might also be plain. (Detachable *manches*, or "sleeves," are sometimes mentioned, but this probably refers to cuffs.) The *capot*'s most distinctive feature was its large hood, affording excellent protection against the elements, especially in winter; some hoods may have been detachable.

In the 1660s Montreal volunteers were nicknamed "*les capots bleus*," but there was no official uniform. While Canadian clothing was occasionally issued to militiamen right up to the end of the French regime, no specific color was prescribed, and records show that colors used by settlers varied widely. Probate records of settlers for the years 1650–1715 mention 232 *capots*; of these, 52.1 percent were blue, 10.3 percent white, 9.9 percent blue and red, 9 percent gray, 6 percent brown, 5.6 percent red, and the rest combined red and white or brownish red, with only 0.04 percent each black, green, buff, olive, "cinnamon," or "musk." Records for 1745–63 mention 85 *capots*, of which 28.2 percent were blue, 27 percent brown, 11.7 percent white and the same number gray, 9 percent black, 7 percent red or wine-red, 2.3 percent green, and 2.3 percent cinnamon. The notion sometimes seen in Canadian histories that blue, white, and red "uniforms" identified Montreal, Trois-Rivières, and Quebec militiamen, respectively, must be dismissed as unfounded.

Some leather *capots* were recorded, but it is clear that wool cloth was usually preferred and seemingly more valuable. Leather garments were seen as utilitarian items and probably used until worn out, so little evidence survives. Trade-store records mention *capots* in white, red, violet, light blue, and green amongst colors offered to First Nations in exchange for furs. Trade blankets could also be used to make what Anglo-Americans came to call "blanket coats"; such *capots* were usually tailored to show the contrasting stripes of the blanket at the lower skirt and sleeves.

To gather the *capot*, a woolen waist-sash was tied over it. This was generally of a single color, usually red, black, green, or brown, though sashes obtained from the First Nations were decorated with quill- or beadwork. (The multicolored cloth "Assumption" sashes only appeared after the end of the French regime.) A long-sleeved, single-breasted, collarless, thigh-length waistcoat (*veste*), as usually worn beneath the European *justaucorps*, might also be worn with the *capot* in winter. Alternatives were a waist-length *gilet*, or a sweater-like *camisole*.

Knee-breeches of light material in summer, of cloth lined with soft leather in winter, and long knitted or woven cloth stockings might be worn. Often, however, the lower garments worn by Canadians and even soldiers in the field were Indigenous. The breechclout – a rectangle of cloth which passed between the legs and hung down front and back over a supporting belt – was popular with Canadian raiders during the warm seasons (see Plate B3). The *mitasses* were long leggings, originally of fringed deerskin but now often of trade cloth sometimes edged with contrasting ribbon or tape. They were held up by knee garters, often decorated in Indigenous style, and also by side thongs to a waist belt if worn with a breechclout.

The moccasins were soft deerskin shoes without heels. Summer moccasins were usually worn over bare feet; winter versions were made of stouter leather, and were larger to accommodate ankle-length, slipper-like cloth *nipes* for warmth. Canadians were also fond of "boot-moccasins," extending most of the way up the calf, in both summer and winter versions. Knitted gloves

"Équipage des Chasseurs Sauvages Canadiens." This matching drawing gives a rare contemporary view of an Indigenous hunting party of *c.*1730; summer raiders might present a very similar appearance. They wear blankets over both shoulders, fastened at the breast and gathered at the waist. The warrior on the left is armed only with a bow, the others with long-barreled muskets. Note powder horns slung on cords to the left hip (left & center), and bullet bags and a tomahawk (right) tucked under the sashes. All three are barefoot, and wear their hair long and loose, as was the Abenaki custom; again, two are smoking pipes. (Courtesy Beinecke Library, Yale University, New Haven, CT; object 1004504)

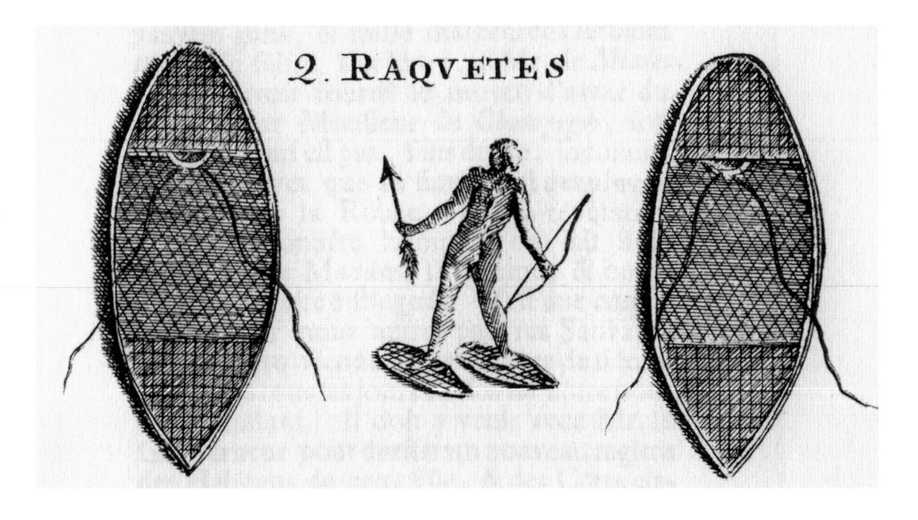

Snowshoes, 1680s; these "*raquetes*" are of the wider, more rounded type worn in deep snow. The European artist/engraver's rendering of a warrior wearing them while naked is unconvincing; Indigenous peoples wore heavy winter clothing. (Print after La Hontan's 1705 Amsterdam edn; author's photo)

could be worn in chilly weather, but mittens were required in winter – made either of cloth or deer, raccoon or seal hide. The mitts were often united by a long thong around the neck and shoulders, since to lose one might condemn a man to disabling frostbite. Moose hide was considered the best material for extreme cold-weather clothing and mitts, and Beauchêne writes that such hides traded from the First Nations were made into winter clothing in several parts of Canada.

By the late 17th century Indigenous warriors (see Plate D) were already using much trade-cloth clothing, including linen shirts. In temperate weather they went lightly dressed, usually in only a shirt perhaps with a sash, breechclout, *mitasses*, and moccasins. Before combat they would often strip almost naked except for moccasins and breechclouts, and daub

This unsigned oil painting is one of very few contemporary renderings of Canadian costume, 1710–30. A detail from an *ex-voto* painting whose colors have degraded over the years, it shows two dead men with the surviving third man giving thanks to Notre-Dame-de-Liesse. The scene might be related to deaths of militiamen. All three wear the *capot*, the two in the foreground (with boot cuffs) entirely brown including buttons, and the third gray. The sashes are green (left) and reddish hues for the others; breeches are brown (left) and red (right), and boot-moccasins are also shown. Parts of two muskets are seen lying on snow, which suggests the late fall or early spring. (Church of Rivière-Ouelle, Quebec, *in situ*; photo courtesy André Gousse)

1720s: First Nations warriors with a Canadian officer, or possibly a chief who has been presented with European clothing. He wears a cocked hat and *justaucorps* coat with *mitasses* and moccasins. At right, note the blanket worn over both shoulders, and the fringed breechclout. (Detail from print in Le Beau's *Voyages curieux et sauvage*, 1738; Library and Archives Canada, NL16410)

themselves with bold areas of war-paint to enhance their tattoos in creating a terrifying appearance. For winter raids they were generally dressed and equipped like the Canadians, though their clothing tended to be somewhat more colorful: La Hontan notes that some decorated their *capots* with beads. Records of 1743 mention that 70 cloth *capots* trimmed with false-silver lace were sent to trade for furs at Fort La Baye (Green Bay). Eight of these were specified as being of white cloth, but the others' colors are not described. The same document lists pairs of cloth *mitasses*: some white, some violet, some blue, and some red and trimmed with silk edging (Monière, LAC micro M-849).

In late spring, summer and early fall, Canadian or regular raiders wore a cap of lighter material or a bandana, a linen shirt, a shorter *capot* that might be of lighter material, a sash, breeches or breechclout, *mitasses* and moccasins. In summer, which could be torrid in southern Canada, the *capot* might be laid aside for just the shirt with a waist-sash. No matter what their order of dress, regular and militia officers wore a crescent-shaped gilded gorget usually engraved with the royal arms, on a ribbon or cord around the neck, as the badge of their status (see Plate B1). Versions of these were sometimes presented to Indigenous chiefs.

Weapons

The three *Compagnies franches de la Marine* that landed at Quebec city in November 1683 had matchlock muskets. Correspondence of 1685 mentions barrels about 119cm (46.8in) long. The caliber was initially rather light, at "20 balls to the pound" (16mm caliber – the old French pound equaled 489mg), but was soon stabilized at "18 balls to the pound" (16.5mm).

The cumbersome matchlocks were soon replaced with lighter and more practical flintlocks. From the early 1690s the Tulle factory became the quasi-exclusive supplier of firearms to the French Navy, made to specifications issued by the Ministry of the Navy (successive models are illustrated and described in Plate H). From 1743, Tulle muskets were made with three iron barrel-bands replacing the previous fixing pins. They were thus very similar to the Army's Model 1728 musket, and the Navy increasingly ordered Army muskets, improved with steel ramrods from 1741. From 1743, muskets issued in Canada were to be marked *Au Roy* ("The King's"), with the mark of the company's captain on the butt. The old plug bayonet, whose narrow handle fitted into the barrel's muzzle, was replaced in Canada between 1721 and 1725 with socket bayonets. Those made for Tulle muskets initially had a noticeable shank about 10.8cm (4.2in) long between the socket and a triangular, guttered blade about 24cm (9.4in) long. Conventional bayonets with a longer blade and almost no shank became common during the 1740s.

Canadian settlers and First Nations warriors always preferred lighter flintlocks. Probate records indicate this from the 1650s on, but there is practically no descriptive data until 1696. That year Tulle contracts specified hunting muskets of a light caliber at "28 to the pound" (14mm), with barrels 121.8cm (47.6in) long, reducing to 113.6cm (44.5in) from 1716 onwards. The furnishings might be of iron or more expensive

H

WEAPONS

The firearms used by raiders were not usually the standard issues of the metropolitan French Army, but weapons ordered by the Navy Ministry for shipboard marines, or made specially for hunting and trading.

Long arms (1)–(5) are drawn approximately to scale:

(1) 1696 Navy *ordinaire* infantry musket made at Tulle, used into the early 18th century. Initially the barrel was 121.8cm long (47.6in) but was shortened to 119cm (46.5in) from 1697 to 1716; the caliber was 16.5mm. Ramrods were of wood with a steel tip. Plug bayonets were used in Canada until 1721–25, when they were gradually replaced with socket bayonets.

(2) 1716 Navy musket made at Tulle, with a single barrel-band and sling rings. Slings *à la grenadiere* were henceforward standard for all muskets. The barrel length was now 113.6cm (44.7in).

(3) 1729 or 1734 contract Navy musket made at Tulle, and used well into the mid-century. Note that the barrel from the breech forward to a molded ring was octagonally faceted; barrel length now reverted to 119.8cm (46.8in).

(4) 1743 Navy muskets made at Tulle became almost identical to the Model 1728 Army musket, with three barrel-bands added to replace the pins securing barrel to stock. Ramrods were all-steel from 1741 onwards.

(5) The hunting muskets preferred by Canadians and traded to Indigenous warriors imitated the Tulle 1716 and 1729/1734 contracts, also later made at Saint-Étienne. Barrel lengths followed successive military specifications (here, 113.6cm/44.7in) but were usually of 14mm caliber. The furniture was usually of iron, but some high-quality examples like this one had fancier brasswork: **(5a)** top view of buttplate, **(5b)** bottom view of trigger guard, **(5c)** lock counter-plate.

Hand weapons (6)–(10) are drawn approximately to scale:

(6) 1729/1734 contract Navy pistol made at Tulle. The basic features of this solid and dependable weapon were little changed between the late 17th century and the 1760s. The barrel is 30.5cm (12in) long, and all the furniture is of iron; note the belt-hook on the left side.

(7) Along with blankets, *boucheron* ("butcher") knives were a basic trade item, used by Canadians and First Nations alike, who might carry as many as three per man. (It is recorded that a militiaman named Cardinal once used a garter-knife to kill an Iroquois.) This 23.6cm (9.3in) example is apparently marked for the French manufacturer Barthélémy Doron; its boxwood hilt has windings of copper wire, and the pommel has been carved into a pig's-head shape.

(8) Mid-18th century knife and sheath also possibly manufactured by Doron, but locally decorated in First Nations style with sewn quillwork and beads.

(9) While soldiers were issued the straight-blade infantry swords, these were not used by raiders, though cutlasses or sabers seem sometimes to have been carried. More ubiquitous was the tomahawk, useful both in combat and as an everyday tool. They were made in both France and Canada, and sometimes bore a stamped lily mark. This typical *casse-téte* ("head-breaker") may be either French- or Canadian-made.

(10) Elaborately decorated and voided head of a French-made pipe-tomahawk, marked "A. Kepoivrer F. P. Lecompte 1761."

(Russel Bouchard, *Les armes à feu en Nouvelle-France* (Septentrion, Quebec;1999); René Chartrand, *French Arms and Armor in America 1503–1783* (Mowbray, Woonsocket, RI; 2016); Kevin Gladysz, *The French Trade Gun in North America 1662–1759* (Mowbray, Woonsocket, RI; 2011); Kevin Gladysz & Ken Hamilton, "French Knives in North America" in *Journal of the Early Americas* (December 2011/January 2012), and "Axes in New France" in *Journal of the Early Americas* (December 2012/January 2013); ANQQ, Génaples, no. 1622)

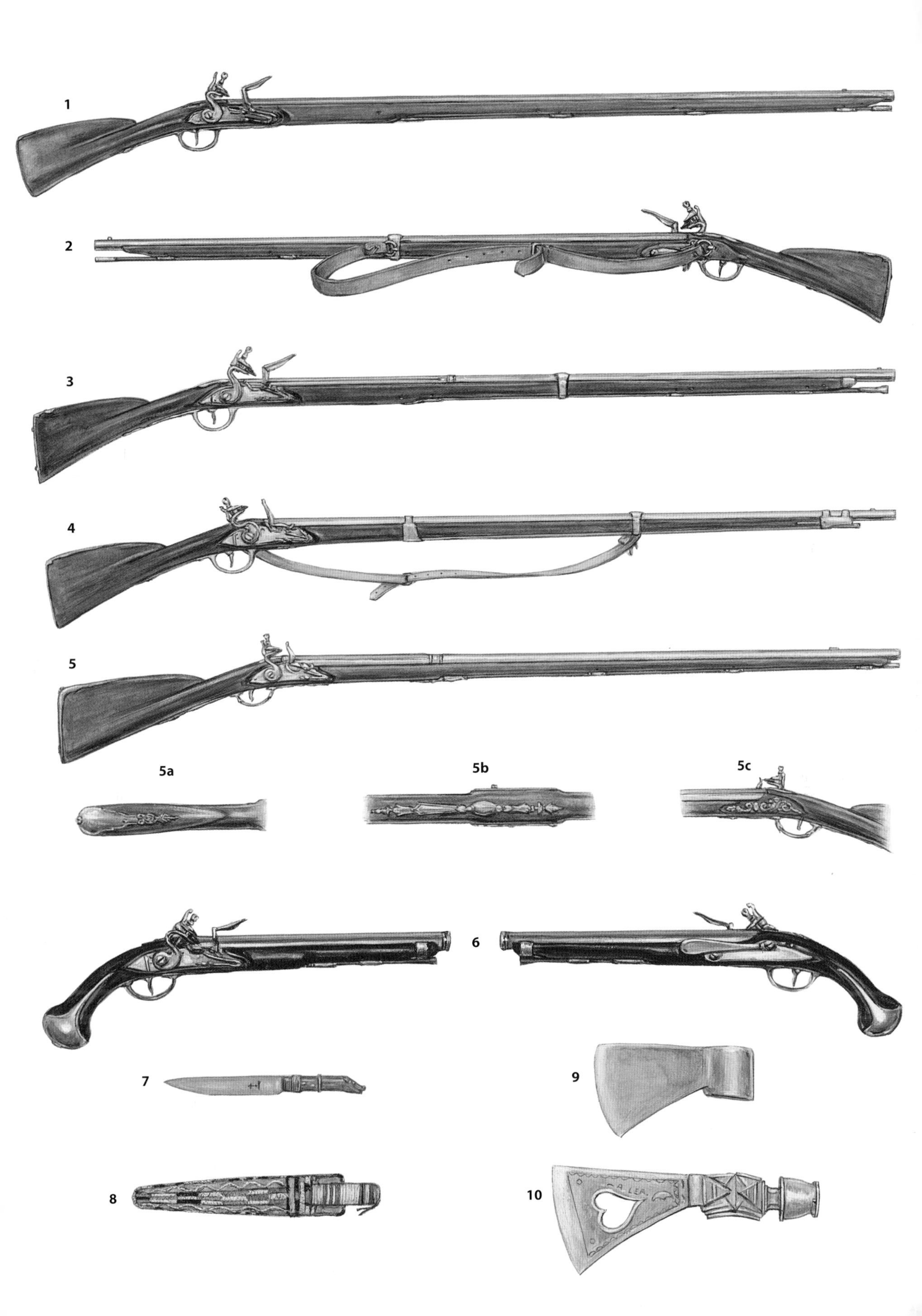

1
2
3
4
5
5a
5b
5c
6
7
8
9
10

brass. Probate records also occasionally reveal "buccaneer" muskets with long barrels, and even a few rifled carbines, but hunting muskets were the overwhelming favorite among the expert Canadians. The trade muskets shipped over for the First Nations were usually similar, although they might be fitted with somewhat fancier brass furniture for added "customer appeal."

Canadian militiamen, and even some soldiers, usually had three knives: one at the waist belt, a smaller one suspended from the neck to hang on the breast, and another on a *mitasse* garter. Pistols, especially for officers, are sometimes mentioned, as are "swords," the latter actually being sabers or naval cutlasses. Tomahawks, which came in several slightly varying types, were the raiders' favorite edged weapon. First Nations warriors carried basically the same weapons as Canadians, but with more variations.

Mounting a raid

As mentioned above regarding the 1686 raid, logistics were vital in wilderness expeditions. Raiders had to rely on what they carried with them in order to survive in forests where game was usually scarce. Ideally, food, tools, weapons, and ammunition were loaded on canoes or toboggans, and on the way out caches were hidden along the route for the return journey. The food was nourishing: mostly corn and dried peas, dried meat, and hard biscuits, though with fortifying shots of brandy.

For winter raids the party would put on snowshoes to travel easily over snow, pulling toboggans with food, arms, and ammunition, and carrying the musket in its protective cloth sleeve. January or February temperatures might fall to between 5°F and -31°F (-15°C and -35°C), with strong, icy winds. A man standing sentry, especially at night, might rapidly suffer serious frostbite.

When the party landed to make its final approach march on the objective, the canoes were hidden. From then on, the journey was made on foot, each man carrying his own pack and weapons. No fires or pipes were lit, and strict silence was imposed, giving the raiders the best chance of arriving within sight of the enemy target without having been detected. Snowshoes would be taken off before the surprise attack was launched, preferably under cover of night or bad weather. The fighting would be fast and ruthless; shocked defenders or settlers were often shot or cut down in a matter of moments, with their houses set ablaze above their heads.

After gathering up booty, the party's return march had to be swift, in spite of any accompanying prisoners, and the journey was utterly exhausting. ("When they come back, they are unrecognizable

Since this contemporary unsigned sketch from the first half of the 18th century is inscribed *"Indiens du Canada,"* it must have been made by a Canadian or a Frenchman in New France. The two nearly naked warriors are obviously in summer dress; the figure on the left may be a chief (*sachem*), while note that the other carries a European saber. (Library of Congress)

There is nothing anachronistic for our period – not even the chair – in this 19th-century print of a Canadian woodsman in winter clothing repairing one of his snowshoes. Note the characteristic fastening of his *capot* to one button at the upper right of the breast. (Private collection; author's photo)

and need a lot of time to recover" – *Relation par lettres...*). It was to be expected that Anglo-American militiamen would pursue the retreating party. Any seriously wounded raiders who could not be brought back were left to die or to be killed by the pursuers; practically no such casualties are known ever to have survived. Once in the wilderness, however, the pursuers too faced danger, because New France raiders had often previously identified good spots to set ambushes (see Plate E).

Prisoners and scalp bounties

This darker side of wilderness warfare cannot be ignored. Scalping had been practiced by First Nations warriors since time immemorial, and the historian of the Abenaki writes that scalps were much-prized war trophies. Early 17th-century Europeans were initially horrified by this practice, but by the end of that century Anglo-American colonists, in particular, had turned scalps into a gruesome commodity.

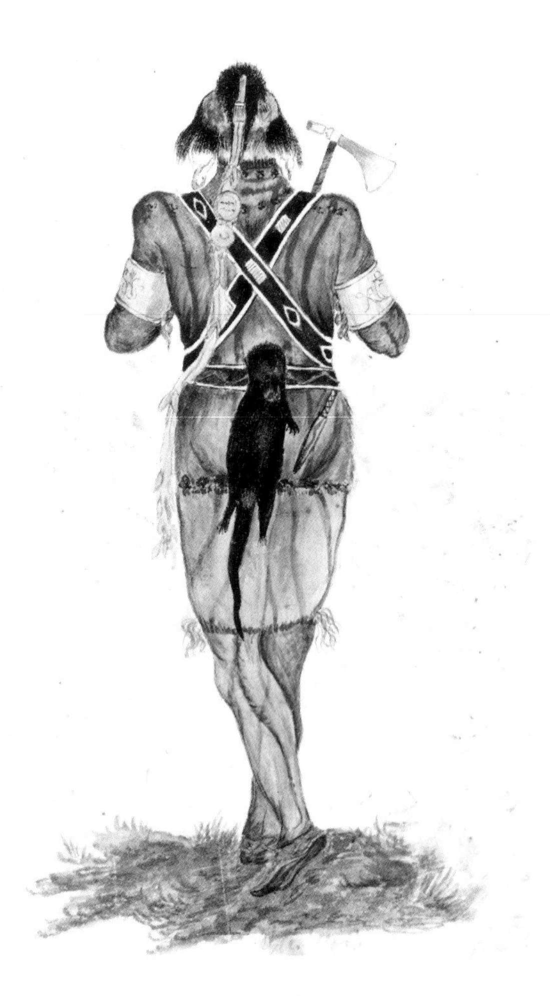

Back view of a Woodlands warrior, 18th century. He carries a pipe-tomahawk, and a small knife hangs from his belt to the right of the pelt of a furred animal. Note the quilled or beaded "bandoliers," the silver armlets, and the elaborate ornament handing from the scalp-lock. (Courtesy Library and Archives Canada, C108983)

During the 1690s the legislatures of both Massachusetts and New Hampshire offered cash bounties of £40 for each enemy warrior's scalp or for a prisoner ten years old or above, and £20 for younger captive children. In 1706, according to Penhallow, the prices paid per scalp by Massachusetts were £10 to regular soldiers; £20 to volunteers on service; £50 to volunteers serving without pay; and £30 to "any troops or company that go to the relief of a town or garrison." The authorities also paid "benefit" for captive women, and children under 12 years old. By 1746, however, Massachusetts had extended the bounties to include any inhabitants of French origin in Canada, and offered £19 for "every scalp of such female or male" children and £20 for those taken prisoner; scalps of "every male" of above 12 years old were worth £38, but adult live prisoners only £40 (Drake). With such narrow margins between the dead or the living, these bounties were in fact an invitation to systematically kill Indigenous, Canadian or French captives of all ages and both sexes.

Since they had virtually no chance of receiving quarter themselves, Indigenous raiders from New France adopted much the same practices, although First Nations warriors all had a traditional preference for taking prisoners over outright killing and scalping. (The pressure on their population numbers was always dangerously high, and in this sense captives who might be adoptable were an economic resource.) Canadian woodsmen were also familiar with scalping, but did not practice it widely. In the late 17th century Canadians had even burned a few Iroquois warriors at the stake in revenge for settlers who had suffered that hideous fate, but they soon ceased a practice that proved useless as a deterrent. While the prospect of such a death was the ultimate horror for Europeans, it was seen by the warriors as the ultimate act of bravery and defiance.

The authorities in New France were much less likely to pay attractive amounts for scalps. There are a few references from Anglo-American colonists of French governors offering scalp bounties, but when they did so it was usually at the behest of the converted "Praying" warriors, who wanted some compensation. On the whole, according to historian Cornelius Jaenen, the French paid as little as one-tenth the bounty offered by the Anglo-Americans; for all their alleged "barbarism," the French in Canada were more inclined to pay handsomely for prisoners and next to nothing for scalps. (The philosopher Henry David Thoreau mentioned one John Lovewell, whose "scalp was worth nothing, since the French Governor offered no bounty for such.")

Many Anglo-Americans were kidnapped during raids by warriors and brought back to Indigenous villages in Canada, where some were certainly put to death, but others enslaved or even adopted. However, in New France there was a system by which officers would buy New England captives from the warriors, which saved many lives. According to MacLeod, in the 18th century a live prisoner could be sold for up to 140 *livres* compared to only 33 *livres* paid for a scalp, and in 1756 offers of up to 1,000 *livres* for a captive are recorded. The most valuable were captured African Americans, who commanded prices of anywhere between 600 and 1,500 *livres* (presumably as slaves).

Redeemed white captives were then brought to Montreal or Quebec City, where there was a detention center to house them until they could be exchanged. According to Norton in 1747, this large "guard-house" held well over a hundred persons – in 1746, as many as 240. Many of these thoroughly traumatized captives later published their experiences, with graphic descriptions of cruelty at the hands of warriors, and, occasionally, some gratitude to the officers who had negotiated their release. Since there were few Canadian or French prisoners in New England, exchanges could take a long time, and Norton mentions that some redeemed New Englanders had been waiting there for "near sixteen month." They were fed, clothed, and might even have social contacts, although language was obviously a barrier. They were not strictly guarded, and "had the free liberty of exercise of our religion, which was a matter of comfort to us in our affliction." Some of the captives eventually even chose to remain in New France and integrated into Canadian society.

By contrast, the fleeting references to them suggest that few Canadian prisoners ever survived capture by Iroquois raiders. The disparity in the bounties offered makes it clear that death was almost always the fate of captured raiders and kidnapped settlers from New France.

Impression of captive Anglo-American settlers being taken back to Canada after a raid. Though such unfortunates suffered severely, a proportion of them survived, and might eventually be exchanged, thanks to French officers who routinely ransomed them from their Indigenous captors. The authorities in New France always offered much higher bounties for live prisoners than for scalps; the same could not be said of those in New England, where very few Canadian captives taken by the Iroquois survived. (Print in Lawler's *Essentials of American History*, 1902; author's photo)

SELECT BIBLIOGRAPHY

Much of the information presented in this modest study was found in France's Archives des Colonies (AC), particularly in series C11A, B and F1A. The original documents are at the Archives Nationales' center for overseas archives at Aix-en-Provence, with copies at Library and Archives Canada (LAC) in Ottawa, and at the Library of Congress (LC) in Washington, DC. The Archives Nationales du Québec (ANQ) at Montreal, Trois-Rivières and Québec City have the probate documents. For the guidance of specialized readers, we occasionally give a short reference in the text, e.g. (C11A, 14), meaning Archives des Colonies series C11A, volume 14. Additional sources are listed with the commentaries to most of the color plates.

Acts and Resolves ... of the Province of Massachusetts Bay ... 1692–1702 (Boston; Wright & Potter, 1892)

Back, Francis, "Le capot canadien..." in *Canadian Folklore Canadien*, Vol. 10, No. 1–2 (1988)

Bacqueville de La Potherie, Claude-Charles, *Histoire de l'Amérique septentrionale...* 4 vols (Paris; Nion & Didot, 1722)

Barbeau, Marius, "Indian Captives" in *Proceedings of the American Philosophical Society*, Vol. 94, No. 6 (December 1950)

Baugy, Louis Henry, Chevalier de, *Journal d'une expédition contre les Iroquois en 1687* (Ernest Sérigny, ed.; Paris; E. Leroux, 1883)

Bearor, Bob, *Leading by example: Partisan Fighters & Leaders of New France 1660–1760,* 3 vols (Bowie, MD; Heritage, 2002)

Beauchêne, *Aventures du chevalier de Beauchêne, Canadien français élevé chez les Iroquois et qui devint capitaine de flibustiers* (1732; republished Paris, Librairie commerciale et asiatique, 1969)

J.C.B. [Joseph Charles Bonin], *Voyage au Canada fait depuis l'an 1751 jusqu'en l'an 1761* (Paris; Aubier, 1978)

Bélisle, Michel, *Sainte-Anne-de-Bellevue 1703–2003* (Sainte-Anne-de-Bellevue; Paroisse, 2003)

Chartrand, René, *French Military Arms and Armor in America 1503–1783* (Andrew Mowbray Inc Publishers; Woonsocket RI, 2016)

von Clauzewitiz, Carl, *De la Guerre* (Paris; Minuit, 1955)

Colden, Cadwallader, *The History of the Five Indian Nations of Canada* (London; T. Osborne, 1747)

Colonial Wars of America 1512–1763, An encyclopedia (Alan Galay, ed; New York & London; Garland, 1996)

Daviaut, Pierre, *Le baron de Saint-Castin, chef abénaquis* (Montréal; ACF, 1939)

Dickason, Olive Patricia, *Canada's First Nations* (Toronto; Oxford University Press, 1997)

Dollier de Casson, François, "Histoire de Montréal," in *Mémoires de la Société historique de Montréal*, quatrième livraison (Montreal, 1868)

Drake, Samuel G., *A Particular History of the Five Years French and Indian War in New England and Parts Adjacent* (Albany; Joel Munsell, 1870)

Dechêne, Louise, *Le Peuple, l'État et la Guerre au Canada sous le Régime français* (Montreal; Boréal, 2008)

Dictionary of Canadian Biography (Quebec, Université Laval, & Toronto, University of Toronto; formerly printed and now online at: http://www.biographi.ca/en/index.php)

The Documentary History of New York, 4 vols (E. B. O'Callaghan, ed; Albany, 1849)

Edmunds, R. Joseph & Joseph L. Peyser, *The Fox Wars* (Norman; University of Oklahoma Press, 1993)

Germain, George-Hébert, *Les Coureurs des bois* (Montreal; Libre-Expression, 2003)

Girouard, Désiré, *Le vieux Lachine et le massacre du 5 août 1689* (Montreal; Gebhardt-Berthiaume, 1889)

Gousse, Suzanne and André, *Costume in New France from 1740 to 1760, A Visual Dictionary* (Chambly; La Fleur de Lyse, 1997)

Baron de La Hontan, Louis-Armand de Lom d'Arce, *Voyages du baron de La Hontan dans l'Amérique septentrionale* (Amsterdam; François L'Honoré, 1705)

Jaenen, Cornelius J., *Friend and Foe* (Toronto; McClelland and Stewart, 1976)

MacLeod, D. Peter, *The Canadian Iroquois and the Seven Years War* (Toronto; Dundurn, 1996)

Maurault, J. A., *Histoire des Abénakis* (Sorel; Gazette, 1866)

Myrand, Ernest, *1690: Sir William Phips devant Québec* (Quebec; Beauchemin, 1893)

A Narrative of an Attempt Made by the French of Canada upon the Mohaques Country being Indians under the Protection of their Majesties Government of New-York (New York; William Bradford, 1693)

Les officiers des troupes de la marine au Canada 1683–1760 (Marcel Fournier, ed; Quebec; Septentrion, 2017)

Penhallow, Samuel, *The History of the Wars of New England with the Eastern Indians…* (Boston; T. Fleet, 1726)

Relation par lettres de l'Amérique septentrionale (années 1709 et 1710) (Camille de Rochemonteix, ed; Paris; Letouzey et aîné, 1904)

Stanley, George F. G., *New France: the last phase 1744–1760* (Toronto; McCleland and Stewart, 1968)

INDEX

Note: page numbers in bold refer to illustrations, captions and plates.